The Quotable Gardener

By Charles Elliott

The Quotable Gardener
The Gap in the Hedge
The Transplanted Gardener

The Quotable Gardener

Edited By
Charles Elliott

metro

First published in the United States of America in 1999 by
The Lyons Press

Published in Great Britain in 2000 by Metro Books (an imprint of Metro
Publishing Limited), 19 Gerrard Street, London W1V 7LA

British Library Cataloguing in Publication Data.
A CIP record of this book is available on request from the British Library.

ISBN 1 900512 88 2

10 9 8 7 6 5 4 3 2 1

Design and composition by Alexander Graphics, Plainfield, IN, USA
Printed in Great Britain by CPD Group, Wales

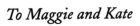

To Maggie and Kate

Contents

Introduction

What is it about gardeners and words? For a class of people thought to be strictly hands-on, the sort of sunburned spadespersons with a far keener appreciation of geraniums than gerunds, a surprising number turn out to be capable of some of the funniest, most pointed, and all-round entertaining prose I've been privileged to read anywhere. Compiling a collection of gardening quotes becomes a matter of trying to decide where to stop.

As a result, the following lot is anything but comprehensive. A truly all-inclusive assembly would be enormous, and instead of consisting of memorable sentences would need to incorporate whole books. Henry Mitchell, the late lamented author of *The Essential Earthman* and too few other books, is a case in point. He could scarcely write a phrase without creating an instant aphorism; trolling his works for good quotes quickly degenerates into a hopeless process of grabbing every third sentence, which is obviously impractical. You'll find plenty of Mitchell here, but I recommend going back to the originals for more.

There were many other pressures to convert the book into a reader. A few poems yield their point only when presented in full. At paragraph length, Proust is irresistible, and I have not resisted. Dickens's seduction scene in a garden from *Pickwick* is too much of a favorite to omit, while Alexander Pope's hilariously savage attack on topiary deserves, to my thinking, as much space as it needs, and gets it.

This by no means the first compendium of gardening quotes, and it's safe to say that it won't be the last. I am grateful to my predecessors, whose work I shamelessly admit to having grazed in the course of putting this collection together. But it is above all personal, a fairly random roundup of items that I found funny, profound, stimulating, wise, or simply possessed of that undefinable quality that makes them stick in the mind. If anything is missing, it is what I have heard called the "God-wottery" factor, the overly sentimental approach to gardens that was so popular at the close of the nineteenth century.

I have tried to identify the source and date of publication of each of the quotes included, but in spite of help from friends (in particular Deborah Singmaster, to whom all thanks), a handful of mysteries remain. I hope they will be forgiven in the same spirit with which a gardener contemplates a seedling that might be a weed—or something wonderful.

The Quotable Gardener

I

Wisdom

There was a time when I thought that a better title for this section would be "Theology," because a good many of the quotes share with religion the kind of transcendental conviction reserved to believers. Gardeners, clearly, care. But there is absolutely nothing predictable about their beliefs, or about the observations their fixation gives rise to. In fact, if gardening were truly a religion, it would most likely have split long ago into dozens of raging crossgrained sects, busily (perhaps bloodily) arguing over such doctrinal issues as the correct way to build a compost pile.

The best gardening writers are invariably the ones with strong opinions, and at the same time a very clear understanding of their own limitations. This probably arises from long contact with nature; only a fool argues head-on with a drought or a prevalence of aphids. You don't have to spend much time working in a garden to discover how much at the mercy of natural forces we all are. I've noticed that there is a distinct tendency in most gardeners not to get discouraged, but to do their best to contend, even if it means taking unlikely measures. As Henry Mitchell observes, "Nature does not hesitate to interfere with me. So I do not hesitate to interfere with it."

I'm no more fond of profundity than I suspect you are, and by calling this section "Wisdom" I certainly don't mean to suggest that it is filled with "great thoughts." The sort of wisdom I'm talking about here grows naturally out of the practice of gardening. And if it is profound—and I can't deny that some of it is, though some is also perverse—it tends to be expressed in a form that the mind can chew on without being choked. That goes as well for the lighter bits, which I've included purely to entertain.

To lock horns with Nature, the only equipment you really need is the constitution of Paul Bunyan and the basic training of a commando.

S. J. PERELMAN
ACRES AND PAINS (1951)

Gardening is the slowest of the performing arts.

ANONYMOUS

Wherever humans garden magnificently, there are magnificent heartbreaks.

HENRY MITCHELL
THE ESSENTIAL EARTHMAN (1981)

A garden is the interface between the house and the rest of civilization.

GEOFFREY CHARLESWORTH
A GARDENER OBSESSED (1994)

The true gardener must be brutal—and imaginative for the future.

> V. SACKVILLE-WEST
> *MORE FOR YOUR GARDEN* (1955)

There is no ancient gentlemen but gardeners.

> WILLIAM SHAKESPEARE
> *HAMLET* (1601)

A country parson without some knowledge of plants is surely as incomplete as a country parsonage without a garden.

> CANON HENRY ELLACOMBE
> *IN A GLOUCESTERSHIRE GARDEN* (1895)

God gave us memories that we might have roses in December.

> J. M. BARRIE
> *COURAGE* (1922)

There are several different ways to lay out a little garden; the best way is to get a gardener.

KAREL ČAPEK
THE GARDENER'S YEAR
TRANSLATED BY M. AND R. WEATHERALL (1931)

The wise gardener is he whom years of experience have succeeded in teaching that plants, no less than people, have perverse individualities of their own, and that, though general rules may be laid down, yet it is impossible ever to predict with any certainty that any given treatment is bound to secure success or failure.

REGINALD FARRER
MY ROCK GARDEN (1920)

Men are like plants—they never grow happily unless they are well cultivated.

CHARLES-LOUIS DE SECONDAT MONTESQUIEU
LES LETTRES PERSANES (1721)

And I beseech you, forget not to informe yourselfe as dilligently as may be, in things that belong to Gardening.

> JOHN EVELYN (1620–1706)

Who has learned to garden who did not at the same time learn to be patient?

> H. L. V. FLETCHER
> *PUREST PLEASURE* (1949)

Nothing is more completely the child of Art than a Garden.

> SIR WALTER SCOTT
> *ESSAY ON LANDSCAPE GARDENING* (1828)

It is a natural consequence that those who cannot taste the actual fruition of a garden should take the greater delight in reading about one. But the enjoyment next below actual possession seems to be derived from writing on the topic.

> *QUARTERLY REVIEW* (1851)

Fathers, instill into your children the garden-mania.

CHARLES JOSEPH, PRINCE DE LIGNE
COUP D'ŒIL SUR BELŒIL (1781)
TRANSLATED AND EDITED BY BASIL GUY (1991)

Give a man secure possession of a bleak rock, and he will turn it into a garden; give him nine years' lease of a garden, and he will convert it into a desert.

ARTHUR YOUNG
TRAVELS IN FRANCE (1792)

Correct handling of flowers refines the personality.

GUSTIE L. HERRIGEL
ZEN IN THE ART OF FLOWER ARRANGEMENT (1958)

If one were as good a gardener in practice as one is in theory, what a garden would one create!

V. SACKVILLE-WEST
SOME FLOWERS (1937)

If gardening isn't a pleasure for you, chances are the work will merely give you a rotten disposition. If you'd rather be golfing or fishing, get a bumper sticker that says so, and forget gardening.

ELSA BAKALAR
A GARDEN OF ONE'S OWN (1994)

It is in society as in nature—not the useful, but the ornamental, that strikes the imagination.

SIR HUMPHRY DAVY (1778–1829)

Odd as it may appear, a gardener does not grow from seed, shoot, bulb, rhizome, or cutting, but from experience, surroundings, and natural conditions.

KAREL ČAPEK
THE GARDENER'S YEAR
TRANSLATED BY M. AND R. WEATHERALL (1931)

The artist gives us the fair image: the gardener is the trustee of a world of fair living things, to be kept with care and knowledge in necessary subordination to human convenience, and the conditions of his work.

WILLIAM ROBINSON
THE ENGLISH FLOWER GARDEN (1881)

So that for all things out of a garden, either of sallads or fruits, a poor man will eat better, that has one of his own, than a rich man that has none. And this is all I think of, Necessary and Useful to be known upon this subject.

SIR WILLIAM TEMPLE
OF GARDENING (1685)

We must cultivate our garden.

VOLTAIRE
CANDIDE (1758)

There is a dangerous doctrine—dangerous because it precludes endless gardening pleasures—that every plant in the garden should be disease-free, bug-free, hardy to cold, resistant to heat and drought, cheap to buy and available at any garden center.

HENRY MITCHELL
HENRY MITCHELL ON GARDENING (1998)

The essence of a real garden is the insignificance of the garden itself; the soul of the real garden lies in the perfect prosperity of the plants of which it is the home.

REGINALD FARRER
INTRODUCTION TO E. A. BOWLES *MY GARDEN IN SPRING* (1914)

To make a great garden, one must have a great idea or a great opportunity.

SIR GEORGE SITWELL
ESSAY ON THE MAKING OF GARDENS (1909)

In Marche and in Aprill, from morning to night:
in sowing and setting, good huswives delight;
To have in a garden, or other like plot:
to trim up their house, and to furnish the pot.

THOMAS TUSSER
HUNDRETH GOOD POINTES OF HUSBANDRIE (1557)

If a young man with an elementary knowledge of gardening can be found, who wants to learn, is strong, willing and intelligent, it is better to supply most of the brains yourself.

HELENA RUTHERFURD ELY
A WOMAN'S HARDY GARDEN (1903)

If you wish to be happy for a day, get drunk;
If you wish to be happy for a week, kill a pig;
If you wish to be happy for a month, get married;
If you wish to be happy for ever and ever, make a garden.

CHINESE PROVERB

Spinsters . . . should take up gardening as a Distraction from the unavoidable Disappointments and Trials of Life.

LOUISA JOHNSON
EVERY LADY HER OWN FLOWER GARDENER (1842)

I have met a few brilliant exceptions of women gardeners who were striking successes, but they usually express themselves as very disappointed with the work of the majority of women who have rushed into gardening.

UNSIGNED LETTER TO *THE GARDENER'S CHRONICLE* (FEBRUARY 15, 1919)

O amateurs of gardening, be amateurs of humanity also.

CHARLES JOSEPH, PRINCE DE LIGNE
LE COUP D'ŒIL SUR BELŒIL (1781)
TRANSLATED AND EDITED BY BASIL GUY (1991)

So with a garden: if you want a lawn, go all out for it. Make everything else subsidiary to the "lawnness" of your lawn. Any planting that enhances the quality you are trying to achieve is good. Any that detracts or confuses is bad . . . This directness and simplicity demands courage and discipline. All the good gardens I have ever seen, all the garden scenes that have left me satisfied, were the result of just such reticence: a simple idea developed just as far as it could be.

RUSSELL PAGE
THE EDUCATION OF A GARDENER (1962)

Flowers seem intended for the solace of ordinary humanity.

JOHN RUSKIN (1819–1900)

Nobody is fond of fading flowers.

THOMAS FULLER
GNOMOLOGIA (1732)

A house built and a garden to grow never brought what they cost.

ANONYMOUS

Europeans never had agreed about the nature of nature.

LEO MARX
THE MACHINE IN THE GARDEN (1964)

When adolescence is passed the mind becomes, to a great extent, settled, and one acquires a bit of land of one's own. That is the beginning of your real gardener, and it is then that gardeners are made.

H. L. V. FLETCHER
PUREST PLEASURE (1948)

Nature does not complete things. She is chaotic. Man must finish, and he does so by making a garden and building a wall.

ROBERT FROST (1874–1963)

If it moves slowly enough, step on it; if it doesn't, leave it—it'll probably kill something else.

ANONYMOUS

Many things grow in the garden that were never sown there.

THOMAS FULLER
GNOMOLOGIA (1732)

There is material enough in a single flower for the ornament of a score of cathedrals.

JOHN RUSKIN
THE STONES OF VENICE (1851)

Die when I may, I want it said of me by those who know me best, that I always plucked a thistle and planted a flower where I thought a flower would grow.

ABRAHAM LINCOLN (1809–1865)

A house though otherwise beautifull, yet if it hath no Garden belonging to it, is more like a Prison than a House.

WILLIAM COLES
THE ART OF SIMPLING (1656)

We sit in other people's gardens, why not in our own?

MIRABEL OSLER
A GENTLE PLEA FOR CHAOS (1989)

Gardening, reading about gardening, and writing about gardening are all one; no one can garden alone.

ELIZABETH LAWRENCE
THE LITTLE BULBS (1957)

Nature does not hesitate to interfere with me. So I do not hesitate to tamper with it.

HENRY MITCHELL
ONE MAN'S GARDEN (1992)

Love your neighbor, yet pull not down your hedge.

GEORGE HERBERT
OUTLANDISH PROVERBS (1640)

I suppose that for most people one of the darker joys of gardening is that once you've got started it's not at all hard to find someone who knows a little bit less than you.

ALLEN LACY
HOME GROUND (1984)

No man but feels more of a man in the world if he have but a bit of ground that he can call his own. However small it is on the surface, it is four thousand miles deep; and that is a very handsome property.

CHARLES DUDLEY WARNER (1829–1900)

It is something, in whatever place, in whatever corner, to have become the Lord and master even of one single lizard.

JUVENAL
SATIRE III (CA. 100 A.D.)

By the time you have grown two thousand species you could believe that you had exhausted Nature's imaginative variability; by the time you have grown five thousand you realize you never will.

GEOFFREY CHARLESWORTH
THE OPINIONATED GARDENER (1988)

Gardening is civil and social, but it wants the vigor and freedom of the forest and the outlaw.

HENRY DAVID THOREAU (1817–1862)

Good gardening and a quiet life seldom go hand in hand.

CHRISTOPHER LLOYD
IN MY GARDEN (1993)

One for the rook, one for the crow,
One to die and one to grow.

ANONYMOUS

To create a little flower is the labour of ages.

WILLIAM BLAKE
THE MARRIAGE OF HEAVEN AND HELL (1793)

Gardening seems an easy art, for infinitude is almost as well suggested in a small plot as a large one.

ROBERT HARBISON
ECCENTRIC SPACES (1977)

A garden should always look bigger than it really is.

ALEXANDRE LE BLOND
THE THEORY AND PRACTICE OF GARDENING
TRANSLATED BY JOHN JAMES (1712)

By the time one is eighty, it is said, there is no longer a tug of war in the garden with the May flowers hauling like mad against the claims of the other months. All is at last in balance and all is serene. The gardener is usually dead, of course.

HENRY MITCHELL
THE ESSENTIAL EARTHMAN (1981)

Gardening gives one back a sense of proportion about everything—
except itself.

> MAY SARTON
> *PLANT DREAMING DEEP* (1968)

———

I had never "taken a cutting" before . . . Do you not realize
that the whole thing is miraculous? It is exactly as though you
were to cut off your wife's leg, stick it in the lawn, and be greeted
on the following day by an entirely new woman, sprung from the
leg, advancing across the lawn to meet you.

> BEVERLEY NICHOLS
> *DOWN THE GARDEN PATH* (1932)

———

Nature abhors a garden.

> MICHAEL POLLAN
> *SECOND NATURE* (1991)

Though I do not believe that a plant will spring up where no seed has been, I have great faith in a seed. Convince me that you have a seed there, and I am prepared to expect wonders.

HENRY DAVID THOREAU
QUOTED IN *FAITH IN A SEED* (1993)
EDITED BY BRADLEY P. DEAN

A garden was the primitive prison, till man, with Promethean felicity and boldness, luckily sinned himself out of it.

CHARLES LAMB
LETTER TO WILLIAM WORDSWORTH, JANUARY 22, 1830
LETTERS (1978)
EDITED BY E. W. MARR

Lord Illingworth: The story of man began in a garden.
Mrs. Allonby: And ended in revelations.

OSCAR WILDE
A WOMAN OF NO IMPORTANCE (1893)

The very statement that there is but one way of making a garden is its own refutation.

> WILLIAM ROBINSON
> *THE GARDEN BEAUTIFUL* (1907)

Let no one think that real gardening is a bucolic and meditative occupation. It is an insatiable passion, like everything else to which a man gives his heart.

> KAREL ČAPEK
> *THE GARDENER'S YEAR*
> TRANSLATED BY M. AND R. WEATHERALL (1931)

The rules of the garden are the rules of art; the rules of the rock-garden are the more awful rules of Nature herself.

> REGINALD FARRER
> *MY ROCK-GARDEN* (1920)

The first three men in the world, were a Gardiner, a Ploughman, and a Grazier; and if any man object, that the second of these was a murtherer, I desire that he would consider that as soon as he was so, he quitted our profession, and turned builder.

> ABRAHAM COWLEY
> *ON AGRICULTURE* (1661)

I am fonder of my garden for the trouble it gives me.

REGINALD FARRER
MY ROCK-GARDEN (1907)

As for our love of gardens, it is the last refuge of art in the minds and souls of many Englishmen; if we did not care for gardens, I hardly know what in the way of beauty we should care for.

SIR ARTHUR HELPS
COMPANIONS OF MY SOLITUDE (1851)

And the Lord God planted a garden eastward in Eden.

GENESIS II

No class of folk is more keenly aware of how shaky the world is.

HENRY MITCHELL
HENRY MITCHELL ON GARDENING (1998)

A garden is but Nature debauched.

HENRY DAVID THOREAU (1817–1862)

A Gardiner is never rich, yet he is ever raking together.

WYE SALTONSTALL
"THE GARDINER"
PICTURES DRAWN FORTH IN CHARACTERS (1635)

A Flower-Gardner that is naturally curious, ought courteously to satisfy the Curiosity of those that desire to see the Flowers of his Garden; in full confidence that they will not offer to pull any.

FRANCIS GENTIL
THE SOLITARY OR CARTHUSIAN GARDNER (1706)

The art of gardening. In this the artist who lays out the work, and devises a garment for a piece of ground, has the delight of seeing his work live and grow hour by hour; and, while it is growing, he is able to polish, to cut and carve, to fill up here and there, to hope, and to love.

PRINCE ALBERT (1819–1861)

Gardens always mean something else, man absolutely uses one thing to say another.

ROBERT HARBISON
ECCENTRIC SPACES (1977)

One of the attractive things about flowers is their beautiful reserve.

HENRY DAVID THOREAU (1817–1862)

Gardens were before gardeners, and but some hours after the earth.

SIR THOMAS BROWNE
THE GARDEN OF CYRUS (1658)

The best place to seek God is in a garden. You can dig for him there.

GEORGE BERNARD SHAW
THE ADVENTURES OF THE BLACK GIRL IN HER SEARCH FOR GOD (1932)

Imaginary gardens with real toads in them.

MARIANNE MOORE'S DEFINITION OF POETRY
"POETRY"
COLLECTED POEMS (1951)

"We *can* talk," said the Tiger-lily, "when there's anybody worth talking to."

LEWIS CARROLL
THROUGH THE LOOKING GLASS (1871)

Gardens are a form of autobiography.

SYDNEY EDDISON
HORTICULTURE MAGAZINE (AUGUST/SEPTEMBER 1993)

2

Work

I have three calluses on my right hand. One, on the inside of the thumb, is from raking. The second, in the lower middle of the palm, developed as a result of too-vigorous use of a trowel to loosen the soil after removing a batch of moribund sweet williams. The third, at the base of the little finger, is a mystery. I don't know exactly where it came from, but one thing's certain—gardening is to blame. Like the dirty fingernails and the stiff back, those calluses are proof if any is needed that gardening is (or ought to be) hard work.

There has been a lot of talk in recent years about "the low-maintenance garden," which is surely an oxymoron. The great Gertrude Jekyll was scathing about such a thing. She, of course, could afford to be—her massive herbaceous borders were labor-intensive, and back then labor was cheap. But she also recognized that at least half the fun of gardening involved getting your hands dirty. These days most of our gardens are probably low-maintenance by her standards, but I'm pleased to say that nobody has yet figured out a way to create a garden that doesn't, to some extent, involve what Wallace Stevens calls "the law of hoes and rakes."

If one theme in this section is the joys and trials of work in the garden, of the grit in the nitty-gritty, another is the eternal search for somebody able and willing to do the job for you. My favorite example of this pleasant phenomenon is Tristram Shandy's Uncle Toby, splendidly successful in getting his corporal to excavate model battlefields in Toby's kitchen garden while he sat by "chatting kindly." S. J. Perelman was constrained to take stronger measures. So far, in my own case I have found that money does the trick with the boy who comes to mow the lawn, but I'm prepared to go further if necessary.

Few lend (but fools)
Their working Tools.

THOMAS TUSSER
HUNDRETH GOOD POINTES OF HUSBANDRIE (1557)

If you are not able, nor willing to hire a gardener, keep your profits to yourself, but then you must take all the pains.

WILLIAM LAWSON
A NEW ORCHARD AND GARDEN (1618)

All gardeners know better than other gardeners.

ANONYMOUS

I've noticed something about gardening. You set out to do one thing and pretty soon you're doing something else, which leads to some other thing, and so on. By the end of the day, you look at the shovel stuck in the half-dug rose bed and wonder what on earth you've been doing.

ANNE RAVER
DEEP IN THE GREEN (1995)

What shall I learn of beans or beans of me? I cherish them, I hoe them, early and late I have an eye to them; and this is my day's work.

HENRY DAVID THOREAU
WALDEN (1854)

Those who labour in the earth are the chosen people of God, if he ever had a chosen people.

THOMAS JEFFERSON
NOTES ON THE STATE OF VIRGINIA (1787)

If gardeners had been developing from the beginning of the world by natural selection they would have evolved most probably into some kind of invertebrate. After all, for what purpose has a gardener a back? Apparently only so that he can straighten it at times, and say: "My back does ache!" As for legs, they may be folded in different ways; one may sit on the heels, kneel on the knees, bring the legs somehow underneath, or finally put them round one's neck; fingers are good pegs for poking holes, palms break clods or divide the mould, while the head serves for holding a pipe; only the back remains an inflexible thing which the gardener tries in vain to bend. The earthworm also is without a back.

KAREL ČAPEK
THE GARDENER'S YEAR
TRANSLATED BY M. AND R. WEATHERALL (1931)

What a man needs in gardening is a cast-iron back, with a hinge in it.

CHARLES DUDLEY WARNER
MY SUMMER IN A GARDEN (1871)

I am sensibly obliged, my dear Lord, by your great goodness, and am most disposed to take the gardener you recommend, if I can . . . I have a gardener that has lived with me above five-and-twenty years; he is incredibly ignorant, and a mule. When I wrote to your Lordship, my patience was worn out, and I resolved at least to have a gardener for flowers. On your not being able to give me one, I half consented to keep my own; not on his amendment, but because he will not leave me, presuming on my long suffering. I have offered him fifteen pounds a year to leave me, and when he pleads that he is old, and that nobody else will take him, I plead that I am old too, and it is rather hard that I am not to have a few flowers, or a little fruit as long as I live.

> HORACE WALPOLE
> LETTER TO THE EARL OF HARCOURT, OCTOBER 18, 1777
> *LETTERS* (1926)
> EDITED BY WILLIAM HADLEY

The circumstances of gardeners, generally mean, and always moderate, may satisfy us that their great ingenuity is not commonly over-recompensed. Their delightful art is practiced by so many rich people for amusement, that little advantage is to be made by those who practice it for profit.

> ADAM SMITH
> *ON THE NATURE AND CAUSES OF THE WEALTH OF NATIONS* (1776)

Don't wear perfume in the garden—unless you want to be pollinated by bees.

> ANNE RAVER (1949–)

Decorum is the refinement of propriety. It is in order to procure stable-dung for hot-beds; it is proper to do this at all times when it is wanted, but it is *decorous* to have the work performed early in the morning, that the putrescent vapours and dropping litter may not prove offensive to the master of the garden, should he, or any of his family or friends, visit the scene.

JOHN CLAUDIUS LOUDON
ENCYCLOPEDIA OF GARDENING (1822)

Seeds are sowing in some parts where plants ought to be reaping, and plants are running to seed while they are thought to be not yet at maturity. Our garden, therefore, is not yet quite the most profitable thing in the world,; but M. d'A. assures me it is to be the staff of our table and existence.

. . . With great labour, he cleared a considerable compartment of weeds, and when it looked clean and well, and he showed his work to the gardener, the man said he had demolished an asparagus bed! M. d'A. protested, however, nothing could look more like *les mauvaises herbes.*

His greatest passion is for transplanting. Everything we possess he moves from one end of the garden to the other, to produce better effects. Roses take the place of jessamines, jessamines of honeysuckles, and honeysuckles of lilacs, till they have all danced round as far as the space allows.

FANNY BURNEY (MADAME D'ARBLAY)
LETTER TO HER FATHER, 1794
LETTERS (1972–1984)
EDITED BY JOYCE HEMLOW

O stagnant east-wind, palsied mare,
Giddap! The ruby roses' hair
Must blow.

Behold how order is the end
Of everything. The roses bend
As one.

Order, the law of hoes and rakes,
May be perceived in windy quakes
And squalls.

The gardener searches earth and sky
The truth in nature to espy
In vain.

He well might find that eager balm
In lilies' stately-statued calm;
But then

He well might find it in this fret
Of lilies rusted, rotting, wet
With rain.

WALLACE STEVENS
"A ROOM ON A GARDEN"
OPUS POSTHUMOUS (1957)

Gardeners have three weapons to use against summer drought:
mulches, watering pots, and prayers.

TYLER WHITTLE
SOME ANCIENT GENTLEMEN (1965)

Oh, Adam was a gardener, and God who made him sees
That half a proper gardener's work is done upon his
    knees,
So when your work is finished, you can wash your hands
    and pray
For the Glory of the Garden that it may not pass away!

RUDYARD KIPLING
THE GLORY OF THE GARDEN (1911)

There is a psychological distinction between cutting back and pruning. Pruning is supposed to be for the welfare of the tree or shrub; cutting back is for the satisfaction of the cutter.

> CHRISTOPHER LLOYD
> THE WELL-TEMPERED GARDEN (1973)

Trench deep; dig in the rotting weeds;
Slash down the thistle's greybeard seeds;
Then make the frost your servant; make
His million fingers pry and break
The clods by glittering midnight stealth
Into the necessary tilth.

> V. SACKVILLE-WEST
> FROM "AUTUMN"
> THE LAND (1926)

I wish with all my heart that I were a man, for of course the first thing I should do would be to buy a spade and go and garden, and then I should have the delight of doing everything for my flowers with my own hands and need not waste time explaining what I want to somebody else.

> COUNTESS VON ARNIM
> ELIZABETH AND HER GERMAN GARDEN (1898)

A good soil, like good food, must not be either too fat, or heavy, or cold, or wet, or dry, or greasy, or hard, or gritty, or raw; it ought to be like bread, like gingerbread, like a cake, like leavened dough; it should crumble, but not break into lumps; under the spade it ought to crack, but not to squelch; it must not make slabs, or blocks, or honeycombs, or dumplings; but, when you turn it over with a full spade, it ought to breathe with pleasure and fall into a fine and puffy tilth. That is a tasty and edible soil, cultured and noble, deep and moist, permeable, breathing and soft—in short, a good soil is like good people, and as is well known there is nothing better in this vale of tears.

KAREL ČAPEK
THE GARDENER'S YEAR
TRANSLATED BY M. AND R. WEATHERALL (1931)

If the reader has not a clear conception of the rood and a half of ground which lay at the bottom of my uncle *Toby's* kitchen garden, and which was the scene of so many of his delicious hours,—the fault is not in me,—but in his imagination;—for I am sure I gave him so minute a description, I was almost ashamed of it.

When FATE was looking forwards one afternoon, into the great transactions of future times,—and recollected for what purposes, this little plot, by a decree fast bound down in iron, had been destined,—she gave a nod to NATURE—'twas enough— Nature threw half a spade full of her kindliest compost upon it, with just so *much* clay in it, as to retain the forms of angles and indentings,—and so *little* of it too, as not to cling to the spade, and render works of so much glory, nasty in foul weather.

My uncle *Toby* came down, as the reader has been informed, with plans along with him, of almost every fortified town in *Italy* and *Flanders*; so let the Duke of *Marlborough,* or the allies, have set down before what town they pleased, my uncle *Toby* was prepared for them.

His way, which was the simplest one in the world, was this; as soon as ever a town was invested—(but sooner when the design was known) to take the plan of it, (let it be what town it would) and enlarge it upon a scale to the exact size of his bowling green; upon the surface of which, by means of a large roll of packthread, and a number of small piquets driven into the ground, at the several angles and redans, he transferred the lines from his paper;

then taking the profile of the place, with its works, to determine the depths and slopes of the ditches,—the talus of the glacis, and the precise height of the several banquets, parapets, &c.—he set the corporal to work—and sweetly went it on:—The nature of the soil,—the nature of the work itself,—and above all, the good nature of my uncle *Toby* sitting by from morning until night, chatting kindly with the corporal upon past-done deeds,—left LABOUR little else but the ceremony of the name.

LAURENCE STERNE
THE LIFE AND OPINIONS OF TRISTRAM SHANDY (VOL. VI, 1762)

This gentleman loves all that grows—
      Bud, shoot, or bough that blossoms dapple.
He plants the rose and feeds the rose
      And guards the springtime apple;

Has a green thumb; is quick to praise
      The frailest petal in his borders;
Can heal (and with a myriad sprays)
      The peony's disorders.

So what has overtaken him,
    What frenzy set his wits to wander
That he should ravage limb by limb
    The wholesome lilac yonder?

That he should lay the privet low
    And do the vines such treason
That scarce a twig, I think, will show
    Its leaf again this season?

A milder chap was never planned,
    Or one with more decorum
But now the weapon's in his hand
    And branches thick before'm

The self-same madness takes his mind
    That took his mind when he was little
And owned a knife and could not find
    Sufficient sticks to whittle.

PHYLLIS MCGINLEY
"MAN WITH PRUNING SHEARS"
THE LOVE LETTERS OF PHYLLIS MCGINLEY (1954)

The moment trees are in bud and the soil is ready to be worked, I generally come down with a crippling muscular complaint as yet unclassified by science. Suffering untold agonies, I nonetheless have myself wheeled to the side line and coach a small, gnarled man of seventy in the preparation of the seed-bed. The division of labor works out perfectly; he spades, pulverizes and rakes the ground, while I call out encouragement and dock his pay whenever he straightens up to light his pipe. The relationship is an ideal one, and I know he will never leave me as long as the chain remains fastened to his leg.

S. J. PERELMAN
ACRES AND PAINS (1951)

———•••———

Cicely: When I see a spade, I call it a spade.
Gwendolen: I am glad to say that I have never seen a spade. It is obvious that our social spheres have been widely different.

OSCAR WILDE
THE IMPORTANCE OF BEING EARNEST (1895)

Gardening reality is born with a hoe in the hand.

SARA STEIN
MY WEEDS (1988)

What do gardeners do in winter? They accumulate fat.

GEOFFREY CHARLESWORTH
THE OPINIONATED GARDENER (1988)

Having commenced gardening, I study the arts of pruning, sowing and planting; and enterprise everything in that way, from melons down to cabbages. I have a large garden to display my abilities in; and were we twenty miles nearer London I might turn higgler, and serve your honour with cauliflowers and broccoli at the best hand.

WILLIAM COWPER
LETTER TO JOSEPH HILL, 1766
SELECTED LETTERS (1926)
EDITED BY W. HADLEY

By dint of hard work, constant care, and endless buckets of water, he had even become a creator, inventing certain tulips and dahlias which seemed to have been forgotten by nature.

VICTOR HUGO
LES MISÉRABLES (1862)

There is not amongst Men a more laborious Life than is that of a good Gard'ner's.

JOHN EVELYN
KALENDARIUM HORTENSIS (1664)

3

Plantings

Probably more banal comments have been made about roses than about any other flower, possibly any other natural object. "What a pother have authors made with roses!" wrote Nicholas Culpeper, and the situation has hardly improved in the 350 years since then. I find this extraordinary. While I do not share Sir Simon Hornby's reported abhorrence of roses—the president of the Royal Horticultural Society claims to be unable to understand why people plant rose gardens at all—there are plenty of other plants that strike me as worthier of admiration. Peonies, for example. Nevertheless, no anthology of garden quotes could ignore the rose, although I still feel a certain sympathy for Marianne Moore's brilliantly reasoned conclusion to her rose poem: "Your thorns are the best part of you."

Most garden writing deals with particular plants, if only because most modern garden writing is of the how-to variety. Relatively few writers, however, seem capable of rising to the level of memorableness that their subject would seem to demand. One splendid exception is Reginald Farrer, alpine expert extraordinaire, whose grand tome *The English Rock Garden* (1919) is a positive Christmas pudding of over-the-top descriptions (most of which are too long—or too improbable—to be quoted).

Another is the early nineteenth-century poet George Crabbe, who comes across as an authentic old-time tulip fancier.

In any case, in my opinion the best quotes dealing with particular plants are generally neither descriptive nor simple praise, but a sort of by-blow, a statement that gets under the skin of the subject and often says more about the gardener than the growing thing. While it isn't strictly speaking about a plant, for example, it would be hard to match Alexander Pope's demolition of the topiary fad for sheer vigor of wit. On the other hand, D. H. Lawrence's poem about Bavarian gentians unsettlingly opens up a whole wonderful Freudian world of horticultural sexuality. What you won't find in this collection is much in the way of instruction. After all, I suspect that despite his excitement, D. H. Lawrence couldn't tell you how to raise a gentian, or even to keep one alive.

"What a pretty flower, I've never seen one like it; there's no one like you, Oriane, for having such marvelous things in your house," said the Princesse de Parme, who, fearing that General de Monserfeuil might have overheard the Duchess, sought now to change the conversation. I looked and recognized a plant of the sort that I had watched Elstir painting. "I am so glad that you like them; they are charming, do look at their little purple velvet collars; the only thing against them is—as may happen to people who are very pretty and very nicely dressed—they have a hideous name and a horrid smell. In spite of which I am very fond of them. But what is rather sad is that they are dying."

MARCEL PROUST
REMEMBRANCE OF THINGS PAST (THE GUERMANTES WAY, 1920)
TRANSLATED BY C. K. SCOTT MONCRIEFF (1925)

It is amazing to me that nurseries without any exception I can recall send dormant blueberry plants at the end of two weeks of perfect planting weather.

HENRY MITCHELL
THE ESSENTIAL EARTHMAN (1981)

Putting in an asparagus bed is like planting a tree. The hard work comes at the beginning, and you need faith in the future to accomplish it.

ELEANOR PERÉNYI
GREEN THOUGHTS (1981)

An iris likes to sit on the ground the way a duck sits on the water: half in, half out.

ANNE RAVER
DEEP IN THE GREEN (1995)

Momordica—*Cucurbitaceæ*—The Squirting Cucumber. An annual gourd-like plant, with woolly leaves, and yellow flowers, the fruit of which resembles a small cucumber; and which, when ripe, bursts the moment it is touched, scattering its seeds, and the half-liquid, pulpy matter in which they are contained, to a considerable distance. This quality made it a favourite, in gardens, a century ago, when some people were yet in a state of sufficient barbarism to find amusements in the annoyance of others; but it has now deservedly fallen into disrepute, and is seldom grown.

JANE WEBB LOUDON
THE LADIES' COMPANION TO THE FLOWER-GARDEN (1840)

This, this! Is Beauty; cast, I pray, your eyes
On this my Glory! See the Grace, the Size!
Was ever Stem so tall, so stout, so strong,
Exact in breadth, in just proportion, long;
These brilliant Hues are all distinct and clean,
No kindred Tint, no blending Streaks between;
This is no shaded, run-off, pin-ey'd thing,
A King of Flowers, a Flower for England's King:
I own my pride, and thank the favouring Star
Which shed such beauty on my fair *Bizarre*.

GEORGE CRABBE
THE BOROUGH (1810)

There is nothing like the first hot days of spring when the gardener
stops wondering if it's too soon to plant the dahlias and starts
wondering if it's too late.

HENRY MITCHELL
THE ESSENTIAL EARTHMAN (1981)

When [the peony] finally drops from the vase, it sheds its vast petticoats with a bump on the table, all in an intact heap, much as a rose will suddenly fall, making us look up from our book or conversation, to notice for one moment the death of what had appeared to be a living beauty.

V. SACKVILLE-WEST
VITA SACKVILLE-WEST'S GARDEN BOOK (1968)
EDITED BY PHILIPPA NICHOLSON

This winter I have added a new scent to my repertoire. I blush to admit my ignorance: for the first time, I have discovered how deliciously many crocuses smell. I am well aware of why I have taken so long to discover this elementary fact. I have always planted my crocuses outdoors and I have never tried crawling through them.

ROBIN LANE FOX
VARIATIONS ON A GARDEN (1974)

The gardener's autumn begins in March, with the first faded snowdrop.

KAREL ČAPEK
THE GARDENER'S YEAR
TRANSLATED BY M. AND R. WEATHERALL (1931)

For the benefit of all my loving Country-men . . . I shall here publish a Catalogue of Greens to be disposed of by an eminent Town-Gardiner, who has lately applied to me upon this Head. He represents, that for the Advancement of a politer sort of Ornament in the Villas and Gardens adjacent to this great City, and in order to distinguish those Places from the meer barbarous Countries of gross Nature, the World stands much in need of a Virtuoso Gardiner who has a turn to Sculpture, and is thereby capable of improving upon the Ancients of his Profession in the Imagery of Evergreens. My Correspondent is arrived to such Perfection, that he cuts Family Pieces of Men, Women or Children. Any Ladies that please may have their own Effigies in Myrtle, or their Husbands in Horn beam. He is a Puritan Wag, and never fails when he shows his Garden, to repeat that Passage in the Psalms, *Thy Wife shall be as the fruitful Vine, and thy Children as Olive Branches round thy Table.* I shall proceed to his Catalogue, as he sent it for my Recommendation.

Adam and *Eve* in Yew; *Adam* a little shatter'd by the fall of the Tree of Knowledge in the great Storm; *Eve* and the Serpent very flourishing.

The tower of Babel, not yet finished.

St George in Box; his Arm scarce long enough, but will be in a Condition to stick the Dragon by next *April.*

A green Dragon of the same, with a Tail of Ground-Ivy for the present.

N.B. *These two not to be Sold separately.*

Edward the *Black Prince* in Cypress.

A *Laurustine* Bear in Blossom, with a Juniper Hunter in Berries.

A Pair of Giants, *stunted,* to be sold cheap.

A Queen *Elizabeth* in Phylyrea, a little inclining to the Green Sickness, but of full growth.

Another Queen *Elizabeth* in Myrtle, which was very forward, but Miscarried by being too near a Savine.

An old Maid of Honour in Wormwood.

A topping *Ben Johnson* in Lawrel.

Divers eminent Modern Poets in Bays, somewhat blighted, to be disposed of a Pennyworth.

A Quick-set Hog shot up into a Porcupine, by its being forgot a Week in rainy Weather.

A Lavender Pig with Sage growing in his Belly.
Noah's *Ark* in Holly, standing on the Mount; the Ribs a little damaged for want of Water.
A Pair of *Maidenheads* in Firr, in great forwardness.

ALEXANDER POPE
THE GUARDIAN (1713)

It would be idle to deny that those gardens contained flarze in full measure. They were bright with Achillea, Bignonia Radicans, Campanula, Digitalis, Euphorbia, Funkia, Gypsophila, Helianthus, Iris, Liatris, Monarda, Phlox Drummondii, Salvia, Thalictrum, Vinca and Yucca. But the devil of it was that Angus McAllister [Lord Emsworth's head gardener] would have a fit if they were picked.

P. G. WODEHOUSE
BLANDINGS CASTLE (1935)

I am very fond of the Spring-flowering colchicums, but unfortunately slugs are also, and those greedy gastropods and I have a race for who can see the flower-buds first. If I win I go out after dark with an acetylene lamp and a hatpin and spear the little army of slugs making for a tea-party at the sign of the Colchicum.

EDWARD AUGUSTUS BOWLES
MY GARDEN IN SPRING (1914)

Go, lovely Rose,
Tell her that wastes her Time and me,
That now she knows,
When I resemble her to thee,
How sweet and fair she seems to be.

EDMUND WALLER
POEMS (1645)

As sense-bludgeoning as a rose.

DIANE ACKERMAN
A NATURAL HISTORY OF THE SENSES (1990)

The rose is a rose,
And always was a rose.
But the theory now goes
That the apple's a rose,
And the pear is, and so's
The plum, I suppose.

The dear only knows
What will next prove a rose.
You, of course, are a rose—
But were always a rose.

ROBERT FROST
"THE ROSE FAMILY"
COLLECTED POEMS (1930)

Bavarian gentians, big and dark, only dark
darkening the day-time torch-like with the smoking
    blueness of Pluto's gloom,
ribbed and torch-like, with their blaze of darkness
    spread blue
down flattening into points, flattened under the sweep of
    white day
torch-flower of the blue-smoking darkness, Pluto's dark-
    blue daze,
black lamps from the halls of Dio, burning dark blue
giving off darkness, blue darkness, as Demeter's pale
    lamps give off light,
lead me then, lead me the way.

Reach me a gentian, give me a torch
let me guide myself with the blue, forked torch of this
    flower . . .

D. H. LAWRENCE
"BAVARIAN GENTIANS"
THE COMPLETE POEMS OF D. H. LAWRENCE (1929)

Rose is a rose is a rose is a rose.

GERTRUDE STEIN
"SACRED EMILY" (1913)
GEOGRAPHY AND PLAYS (1922)

You do not seem to realize that beauty is a liability
    rather than an asset—that in view of the fact that
        spirit creates form we are justfied in supposing
    that you must have brains. For you, a symbol of the
        unit, stiff and sharp,
    conscious of surpassing by dint of native superiority
        and liking for everything
self-dependent, anything an

ambitious civilization might produce: for you, unaided,
        to attempt through sheer
    reserve, to confuse presumptions arising from
        observation, is idle. You cannot make us
        think you a delightful happen-so. But rose, if you
        are brilliant, it
    is not because your petals are the without-which-
        nothing of pre-eminence. Would you not, minus
thorns, be a what-is-this, a mere

peculiarity? They are not proof against a worm, the
    elements, or mildew;

but what about the predatory hand? What is brilliance
without co-ordination? Guarding the
infinitesimal pieces of your mind, compelling
audience to
the remark that it is better to be forgotten than to be
remembered too violently,
your thorns are the best part of you.

MARIANNE MOORE
"ROSES ONLY"
SELECTED POEMS (1935)

The Golden Glow [*Rudbeckia laciniata*] should be divided every
other year, and in this way it is even more remunerative than the
Phlox. I started with fifty plants, and think it will soon be possible
to have a farm of them.

HELENA RUTHERFURD ELY
A WOMAN'S HARDY GARDEN (1903)

In the door-yard fronting an old farm-house, near the
white-wash'd palings,
Stands the lilac bush, tall-growing, with heart-shaped
leaves of rich green,
With many a pointed blossom, rising, delicate, with the
perfume strong I love,
With every leaf a miracle . . . and from this bush in the
door-yard,
With delicate-color'd blossoms, and heart-shaped leaves of
rich green,
A sprig, with its flower, I break.

WALT WHITMAN
"WHEN LILACS LAST IN THE DOORYARD BLOOM'D"
SEQUEL TO DRUM TAPS (1865–66)

Of all the plants I know, the one whose foliage has the strongest
sound is the Virginian allspice (*Calycanthus floridus*), whose leaves
are of so dry and harsh a quality that they seem to grate and clash
as they come together.

GERTRUDE JEKYLL
HOME AND GARDEN (1900)

I am strongly of the opinion that a quantity of plants, however good the plants may be themselves and however ample their number, does not make a garden; it only makes a collection.

GERTRUDE JEKYLL
COLOUR IN THE FLOWER GARDEN (1908)

Hollyhocks are very aspiring Flowers.

JOHN LAWRENCE
THE FLOWER GARDEN (1726)

Roses do comfort the heart.

WILLIAM LANGHAM
THE GARDEN OF HEALTH (1579)

It is a greater act of faith to plant a bulb than to plant a tree.

CLARE LEIGHTON
FOUR HEDGES (1935)

Who that has a garden and a taste for flowers, would be without the Crocus, the Snowdrop, the Primrose, the Violet, the Cyclamen, Hepatica, Hyacinth, Narcissus, Auricula, Ranunculus, Anemone, Wallflower, Stock, Pink, Tulip, Carnation, Rose, Iris, Lily, Lychnis, Lobelia, Delphinium, Verbascum, Rudbeckia, Anthericum, Aconitum, Monarda, Ferraria, Gentiana, Aenothera, Scilla peruviana, Paeony, Phlox, Hemerocallis, Coreopsis, Campanula, Cina Aster, Hollyhock, and a multitude of others, each species consisting of many beautiful varieties, both single and double.

THOMAS HOGG
A PRACTICAL TREATISE ON THE CULTURE OF THE CARNATION (1839)

Violets smell like burnt sugar cubes that have been dipped in lemon and velvet.

DIANE ACKERMAN
A NATURAL HISTORY OF THE SENSES (1990)

I wish the sky would rain down roses, as they rain down from the shaken bush. They would fall down light as feathers, smelling sweet, and it would be like sleeping and yet waking, all at once.

GEORGE ELIOT (1819–1880)

It is obvious that close planting [of shrubs] gives a furnished look to a border almost immediately; equally obvious that it is wasteful and expensive.

CHRISTOPHER LLOYD
THE WELL-TEMPERED GARDEN (1973)

Whether flowers should or should not be planted at all around a house, is a question of considerable moment, and as a general rule, we must confess, our own judgment is against it.

HENRY WINTHROP SARGENT
*SUPPLEMENT TO THE SIXTH EDITION OF LANDSCAPE GARDENING
BY* ANDREW JACKSON DOWNING (1859)

Dark ages clasp the daisy root.

JAMES JOYCE
FINNEGANS WAKE (1939)

Of al the floures in the mede,
Thanne love I most thise floures white and rede,
Swiche as men callen daysyes in our toun . . .
Allas, that I ne had Englyssh, ryme or prose,
Suffisant this flour to preyse aryght!

GEOFFREY CHAUCER
PROLOGUE TO *THE LEGEND OF GOOD WOMEN* (CA. 1380–1386)

There are some botanical names that are teasers. Where Polish discoverers or Russian explorers come upon the scene the result is apt to be an appalling jungle of horrors. Michaux, Stribnry, Przewalsky, Tchihatchew are responsible for some real jawbreakers; and when it comes to *Michauxia tchihatchewi*, exhausted humanity gives up in despair.

REGINALD FARRER
MY ROCK-GARDEN (1907)

Our attitude towards plants is a singularly narrow one. If we see any immediate utility in a plant we foster it. If for any reason we find its presence undesirable or merely a matter of indifference, we may condemn it to destruction forthwith.

RACHEL CARSON
SILENT SPRING (1963)

Forsythia is pure joy. There is not an ounce, not a glimmer of sadness or even *knowledge* in forsythia.

ANNE MORROW LINDBERGH (1906–   )

There is no doubt whatsoever that I will be outlived by my garlic, and that long after my own genes have been diluted beyond recognition, my bindweed's genes will be the same genes I left behind in my first, failed garden.

SARA STEIN
MY WEEDS (1988)

All the wars of the world, all the Caesars, have not the staying power of a lily in a cottage border.

REGINALD FARRER
THE RAINBOW BRIDGE (1921)

The lilac, before it flowers, when it is still nothing but small leaves like aces of spades and shows promise of becoming a midget thyrsus, the lilac then has a discreet smell of scarab-beetles, right up to the moment when in full flower the sprays foam into white, mauve, blue, and purple, and it drenches suburban trains, undergrounds and children's play-pens with its toxic aroma of prussic acid.

COLETTE
POUR UN HERBIER (1949)
TRANSLATED BY ROGER SENHOUSE AS *FOR A FLOWER ALBUM* (1959)

There is nothing like pruning a grapevine for training oneself to think like a plant.

HUGH JOHNSON
THE GARDEN MAGAZINE (APRIL 1997)

As I do not know the names of all the weeds and plants, I have to do as Adam did in his garden—name things as I find them.

CHARLES DUDLEY WARNER
MY SUMMER IN A GARDEN (1871)

The movement was slower than any animal's, swifter than any plant's I have ever seen before. How can I suggest it to you—the way that growth went on? The leaf tips grew so that they moved onward even while we looked at them. The brown seed-case shrivelled and was absorbed with equal rapidity. Have you ever on a cold day taken a thermometer into your warm hand and watched the little thread of mercury creep up the tube? These moon-plants grew like that.

H. G. WELLS
THE FIRST MEN IN THE MOON (1905)

Do you know what faces [poppies] have—how they peep and peer, and look arch and winning, or bold and a little insolent sometimes? Have you ever noticed their back-hair, how beautifully curled it is?

EDWARD BURNE-JONES
QUOTED IN *MEMORIALS OF EDWARD BURNE-JONES* (1904)
GEORGIANA BURNE-JONES

Theophrastus . . . calleth the Rose the light of the earth, the faire bushie toppe of the spring, the fire of love, the lightning of the land.

JOHN PARKINSON
THEATRUM BOTANICUM (1640)

A pale rose is a smell that has no fountain; that has upside down the same distinction; elegance is not colored, the pain is there.

GERTRUDE STEIN
GEOGRAPHY AND PLAYS (1922)

What a pother have authors made with Roses! What a racket
have they kept!

NICHOLAS CULPEPER
AN ENGLISH HERBAL ENLARGED (1653)

As the immense dew of Florida
Brings forth
The big-finned palm
And green vine angering for life,

As the immense dew of Florida
Brings forth hymn and hymn
From the beholder
Beholding all these green sides
And gold side of greensides,

And blessed mornings
Meet for the eye of the young alligator,
And lightning colors,
So, in me, come flinging
Forms, flames, and the flakes of flames.

WALLACE STEVENS
"NOMAD EXQUISITE"
HARMONIUM (1923)

Quite certain that he would not be recognized, [Prince Genji] leaned out for a closer look. The hanging gate, of something like trelliswork, was propped on a pole, and he could see that the house was tiny and flimsy. He felt a little sorry for the occupants of such a place . . . A pleasantly green vine was climbing a board wall. The white flowers, he thought, had a rather self-satisfied look about them . . .

An attendant came up, bowing deeply. "The white flowers . . . are known as 'evening faces,' " he said. "A very human sort of name—and what a shabby place they have picked to bloom in."

"A hapless sort of flower. Pick one off for me, would you?"

The man went inside the raised gate and broke off a flower. A pretty little girl in long, unlined trousers of yellow silk came out through a sliding door that seemed too good for the surroundings. Beckoning to the man, she handed him a heavily scented white fan.

"Put it on this. It isn't much of a fan, but then it isn't much of a flower, either."

MURASAKI SHIKIBU
THE TALE OF GENJI (CA. 1010)
TRANSLATED BY EDWARD G. SEIDENSTICKER (1976)

When Wordsworth's heart with pleasure filled at a crowd of golden daffodils, it's a safe bet he didn't see them two weeks later.

GEOFF HAMILTON (1936–1996)

Light is the engine of plants.

CHRISTOPHER REED
HORTICULTURE MAGAZINE (AUGUST/SEPTEMBER 1994)

Flower-muscle, that opens the anemone's
meadow-morning bit by bit
until into her lap the polyphonic
light of the loud skies pours down . . .

RAINER MARIA RILKE
SONNETS TO ORPHEUS
TRANSLATED BY M. D. HERTER (1942)

The tulips are too excitable.

SYLVIA PLATH
"TULIPS"
COLLECTED POEMS (1962)

... the little western flower
Before milk-white, now purple with love's wound,
And maidens call it love-in-idleness.

WILLIAM SHAKESPEARE
ON THE PANSY
A MIDSUMMER NIGHT'S DREAM (1600)

Here stood the tulips just ready to flower: still grey and pointed, but brilliantly veined with the crimsons, mauves, yellows they were to be.

ELIZABETH BOWEN (1899–1973)

There is nothing very beautiful about the sunflower; but I am told that it bends towards the sun, which is strange and rather appealing.

SEI SHŌNAGON
THE PILLOW BOOK OF SEI SHŌNAGON (TENTH CENTURY)
TRANSLATED BY IVAN MORRIS (1967)

As for the roses, you could not help feeling that roses are the only flowers that impress people at garden parties; the only flowers that everybody is certain of knowing.

KATHARINE MANSFIELD
"THE GARDEN PARTY"
THE GARDEN PARTY AND OTHER STORIES (1922)

Often some species would entirely capture the garden—forget-me-nots one year, hollyhocks the next, then a sheet of harvest poppies. Mother went creeping about the wilderness, pausing to tap some odd bloom on the head, as indulgent, gracious, amiable and inquisitive as a queen at an orphanage.

LAURIE LEE
CIDER WITH ROSIE (1959)

There is simply the rose; it is perfect in every moment of its existence.

RALPH WALDO EMERSON (1803–1882)

Open afresh your round of starry folds
Ye ardent marigolds.

JOHN KEATS
"I STOOD TIP-TOE UPON A LITTLE HILL"
POEMS BY JOHN KEATS (1817)

Her mother had none of the present snobbish form of gardening, of balancing and landscaping even a small area. She planted exactly where her plants would do best. From this principle there grew the wandering bows and tidy knots of box edging, gardens within gardens, within gardens—Russian dolls in the spaces—spaces skeleton now but ever containing small treasures, whether they flowered in spring, summer or winter: gentian, double white violets, cyclamen, double primroses, saxifrage, Hose-in-Hose, May could see them still with some of the avid perceptions of childhood.

> MOLLY KEANE
> TIME AFTER TIME (1983)

We shall be magnificent in dahlias.

> MARY RUSSELL MITFORD
> LETTER TO EMILY JEPHSON, JULY 4, 1838
> MY GARDEN (1990)

My garden is an honest place. Every tree and every vine are incapable of concealment, and tell after two or three months exactly what sort of treatment they have had.

> RALPH WALDO EMERSON
> JOURNALS (PUBLISHED 1909–1913)

Consider the grasses, so carefully distinguished from one another. They are little figures of speech. *Glastridium*—nit-grass, from *gastridion*, a little swelling. *Aira*—hair-grass, from *airo*, to destroy (a destructive grass). *Panicum*, or panick-grass, from *panis*, bread, because the seeds of this grass can be milled and eaten. *Arrhenatherum* is from *arrhen*, male, and *ather*, an awn. It was the natural grass for me to choose to put into a sentence with the shade of *les jeunes gens en fleur?* And then the vernal grass, *anthoxanthum anthos*, a flower, *xanthos*, yellow, next to *phalaris*—phalos, shining and suddenly, do we have a description, or an evocation of the fields of light?

A. S. BYATT
STILL LIFE (1985)

The haughty thistle o'er all danger towers
In every place the very wasp of flowers.

JOHN CLARE
"FEAR OF FLOWERS"
POEMS CHIEFLY FROM MANUSCRIPT (1920)
EDITED BY EDMUND BLUNDEN AND ALAN PORTER

4

Design

I worry about design. We've been building a garden for more than a decade now. It has grown organically, bit by bit as the notion strikes, rather like a plant luxuriantly stretching itself over the course of a summer. One year I flagged the terrace and built some walls; another year we dug out old rhododendrons and made a long bed; yet another year we made a second perennial bed and planted hedges. There is a pergola now, shrub collections, trees, a cleared space in the wood for forest plants.

All this has been done in the absence of a design plan. I know that this is wrong. Everybody says so. But guilt has yet to drive me to make one. I do feel nervousness about undertaking some new project without having considered the overall design first; the result tends to be procrastination. For example, the flagstones for a new walk across the lawn to the front door are still stacked where they have been for a year, while I mull over the notion of bordering the walk with pleached trees. I like to think that if we had a grand plan, there wouldn't be such uncertainty.

One rainy day last summer I did attempt to make a scaled drawing of the whole place, as a first step toward a proper garden design. Nothing is regular at Towerhill Cottage—few straight lines, no right angles, even the buildings refuse to bear a sensible relation to one another. The ground levels are another problem. But in the end I produced a sort of elementary sketch map showing the house and garden and trees. After looking at it for a while, I put it in a desk drawer, and it is still there.

Since I am unlikely to do anything conclusive about designing our garden—it will be finished first—the best thing may be to stop worrying about it. On the evidence of quotes in this section, plenty of fine gardeners, from Andrew Marvell on, seemed to have regarded formal design as slightly superfluous, if not downright restrictive. I'll go along with William Morris, who says that a garden should look like part of the house. Whatever else it may look like, ours does that.

A little studied negligence is becoming to a garden.

ELEANOR PERÉNYI
GREEN THOUGHTS (1981)

The light and the deep, the red and the white, should be
spaced apart;
The early and the late should likewise be planted in due
order.
My desire is, throughout the four seasons, to bring wine
along,
And not to let a single day pass without some flower
opening.

OU-YANG HSIU (1007–1072)
"ASSISTANT HSIEH PLANTING FLOWERS AT THE SECLUDED VALLEY"
THE PENGUIN BOOK OF CHINESE VERSE (1962)
TRANSLATED BY ROBERT KOTEWALL AND NORMAN L. SMITH

Subjugated gardens abound, and I can see why. Unless discipline
is maintained from the moment the spirit-level is laid across the
earth, you are nourishing a vast, tactile, heavy-scented siren which
will keep you forever in its thrall.

MIRABEL OSLER
HORTUS (1990)

VII. If the Garden has been properly laid out, there need not be a maze in it. For the quest, the puzzlement, the contingency of the place of rest with its bench and rosebushes in the center of it all, the ease of entrance and its welcoming entrapment, the problems of homing, will all have been provided by the Garden itself. And the maze's parable, unrolling beneath the hurrying feet of the last wanderers on a summer evening that now chills and darkens—the parable of how there can be no clarity of truth without puzzlement, no joy without losing one's way—will be propounded by the Garden's final perfection, namely, that in it is no trace of the designer, that no image of him can ever be found. He—you—will have disappeared into the ground of the place that has been made.

JOHN HOLLANDER
"INSTRUCTIONS TO THE LANDSCAPER"
HARP LAKE (1988)

The other kind of boundless garden is not a geometrical figure at all. This English kind has no obvious beginning or end and the bounds are confused on all sides, so that for this garden an un-wall had to be invented, which performs the physical functions without having the visual value of a wall. The ha-ha or sunken fence is an English joke on law and order that exercises real constraint with the English deviousness and we can almost imagine a simple person stumbling into these sophisticated gardens without realizing that he is in a garden at all, like someone who misses an irony.

ROBERT HARBISON
ECCENTRIC SPACES (1977)

Consult the genius of the place in all.

ALEXANDER POPE
"OF THE USE OF RICHES"
EPISTLE TO BURLINGTON (1735)

ART should never be allowed to set foot in the province of nature, otherwise than clandestinely and by night. Whenever she is allowed to appear here, and men begin to compromise the difference—Night, gothicism, confusion and absolute chaos are come again.

WILLIAM SHENSTONE
"UNCONNECTED THOUGHTS ON GARDENING"
THE WORKS IN PROSE AND VERSE OF WILLIAM SHENSTONE, ESQ. (1764)

To talk of a "natural" or "wild" garden is a contradiction in terms. You might as well talk of a natural "zoo," and do away with the bars, and arrange bamboo brakes for the tigers, mountaintops for the eagles, and an iceberg for the polar bears.

EDEN PHILPOTTS
MY GARDEN (1906)

If it came to making my own large Paradise, I have no wish for an eighteenth-century landscape garden. We praise them now too much. There is something enervating in the character of such gardens, something thin, too pictorial, too imitative, too tastefully pretentious . . . A large wind, I feel, might roar through at any moment and burst the canvas and spoil all this careful Claudian illusion.

GEOFFREY GRIGSON
GARDENAGE (1952)

It is unchristian to hedge from the sight of others the beauties of nature which it has been our good fortune to create or secure.

FRANK J. SCOTT
THE ART OF BEAUTIFYING SUBURBAN HOME GROUNDS (1870)

Wild gardening sounds as attractive nowadays as a wild woman or a wild party.

ROBIN LANE FOX
VARIATIONS ON A GARDEN (1986)

I have rarely seen either ruins or rivers well manufactured.

WILLIAM GILPIN
REMARKS ON FOREST SCENERY AND OTHER WOODLAND VIEWS (1834)

What is a garden?
   Goodness knows!
You've got a garden,
   I suppose:

To one it is a piece of ground
For which some gravel must be found.
To some, those seeds that must be sown,
To some a lawn that must be mown.
To some a ton of Cheddar rocks;
To some it means a window box;

To some, who dare not pick a flower—
A man, at eighteen pence an hour.
To some, it is a silly jest
About the latest garden pest;
To some, a haven where they find
Forgetfulness and peace of mind . . .

What is a garden
Large or small
'Tis just a garden,
After all.

REGINALD ARKELL
"WHAT IS A GARDEN"
GREEN FINGERS (1935)

The area of a handsom *Garden* may take up thirty or forty Acres, not more.

PHILIP MILLER
THE GARDENER'S DICTIONARY (1724)

Sources of pleasure in Landscape Gardening:—1, Conformity; 2, Utility; 3, Order; 4, Symmetry; 5, Picturesque Effect; 6, Intricacy; 7, Simplicity; 8, Variety; 9, Novelty; 10, Contrast; 11, Continuity; 12, Association; 13, Grandeur; 14, Appropriation; 15, Animation.

HUMPHRY REPTON
SKETCHES AND HINTS ON LANDSCAPE GARDENING (1794)

Mr Milestone.—Here is another part of the ground in its natural state. Here is a large rock, with the mountain-ash rooted in its fissures, over-grown, as you see, with ivy and moss, and from this part of it bursts a little fountain, that runs bubbling down its rugged sides.

Miss Tenorina.—O how beautiful! How I should love the melody of that miniature cascade!

Mr Milestone.—Beautiful, Miss Tenorina! Hideous. Base, common, and popular. Such a thing as you may see anywhere in wild and mountainous districts. Now, observe the metamorphosis. Here is the same rock, cut into the shape of a giant. In one hand he holds a horn, through which the little fountain is thrown to a prodigious elevation. In the other is a ponderous stone, so exactly balanced as to be apparently ready to fall on the head of any person who happens to be beneath, and there is Lord Littlebrain walking under it.

Squire Headlong.—Miraculous, by Mahomet!

> THOMAS LOVE PEACOCK
> *HEADLONG HALL* (1816)

The garden that is finished is dead.

> H. E. BATES (1905–1974)

Large or small, [a garden] should look both orderly and rich. It should be well fenced from the outside world. It should by no means imitate either the wilfulness or the wildness of Nature, but should look like a thing never to be seen except near a house. It should, in fact, look like a part of the house.

> WILLIAM MORRIS
> *HOPES AND FEARS FOR ART* (1882)

Flowers . . . are richness enough in the garden picture. To add
further ornamentation is to distract.

RUSSELL PAGE
EDUCATION OF A GARDENER (1962)

He therefore who would see his flow'rs disposed
Sightly and in just order, 'ere he gives
The beds the trusted treasure of their seeds
Forecasts the future whole, That when the scene
Shall break into its preconceived display,
Each for itself, and all as with one voice
Conspiring, may attest his bright design.

WILLIAM COWPER
THE TASK (1785)

I have a garden of my own
But so with roses overgrown,
And lilies, that you would it guess
To be a little wilderness.

ANDREW MARVELL
"THE NYMPH COMPLAINING FOR THE DEATH OF HER FAUN"
OCCASIONAL POEMS (1681)

Passion for display appears the ruling note in English horticulture of every kind and in every period: we want a show.

REGINALD FARRER
INTRODUCTION TO E. A. BOWLES' *MY GARDEN IN SPRING* (1914)

Nor am I displeased with the placing of ridiculous Statues in Gardens, provided they have nothing in them obscene.

LEON BATTISTA DEGLI ALBERTI
DE RE ÆDIFICATORIA (1485)
TRANSLATED BY G. LEONE (1726)

Style is a matter of taste, design a matter of principles.

THOMAS CHURCH
GARDENS ARE FOR PEOPLE (1955)

In the blending of different elements, the subtle transition from the fixed and formal lines of art to the shifting and irregular lines of nature, and lastly in the essential convenience and liveableness of the garden, lies the fundamental secret of the the old garden-magic.

EDITH WHARTON
ITALIAN VILLAS AND THEIR GARDENS (1904)

Who loves a garden, loves a green-house too,
Unconscious of a less propitious clime
There blooms exotic beauty, warm and snug,
While the winds whistle and the snows descend.

WILLIAM COWPER
THE TASK (1785)

It is a curious thing that people will sometimes spoil some garden project for the sake of a word. For instance, a blue garden, for beauty's sake, may be hungering for a group of white lilies, or for something of palest yellow, but it is not allowed to have it because it is called the blue garden and there must be no flowers in it but blue flowers . . . My own idea is that it should be beautiful first, and then just as blue as may be consistent with its best possible beauty.

GERTRUDE JEKYLL
COLOUR IN THE FLOWER GARDEN (1908)

All gardening is landscape painting.·

HORACE WALPOLE
ON MODERN GARDENING (1780)

Every approach to irregularity and a wild, confused, crowded, or natural-like appearance must be avoided in gardens avowedly artificial.

JOHN CLAUDIUS LOUDON
ENCYCLOPEDIA OF GARDENING (1822)

Once it has a toehold, incongruity has a way of advancing systematically through the garden like quackgrass.

DES KENNEDY
CRAZY ABOUT GARDENING (1994)

Plans should be made on the ground to fit the place, and not the place made to suit some plan out of a book.

WILLIAM ROBINSON
THE GARDEN BEAUTIFUL (1907)

I fear I am a little impatient of the school of gardening that encourages the selection of plants merely as artistic furniture, chosen for colour only, like ribbons or embroidery silk. I feel sorry for plants that are obliged to make a struggle for life in uncongenial situations because their owner wishes all things of those shades of pink, blue or orange to fit in next to the grey or crimson planting.

EDWARD AUGUSTUS BOWLES
MY GARDEN IN SPRING (1914)

Few seemingly so artless forms of garden design can so quickly slip over into pure kitsch.

ROY STRONG
ON COTTAGE GARDENS
CREATING SMALL GARDENS (1987)

You have only to think of the front gardens you drive past in summer that are planted up almost entirely with dwarfs to realize how lacking in character and individuality they are. Such plants never get off the ground; they are mere colour explosions.

CHRISTOPHER LLOYD
THE WELL-TEMPERED GARDEN (1973)

When smiling lawns and tasteful cottages begin to embellish a country, we know that order and culture are established.

ANDREW JACKSON DOWNING
TREATISE ON LANDSCAPE GARDENING (1841)

"It may seem impertinent of me to praise, but I must admire the taste Mrs. Grant has shown in all this. There is such a quiet simplicity in the plan of the walk! Not too much attempted!"

JANE AUSTEN
MANSFIELD PARK (1814)

First grow cabbages. After that, plant a flower. When you have successfully grown a flower, then you can start to think about growing a tree. After watching a tree grow for several years, observing how its character develops from year to year, then you can begin to think of a composition of living plants—a composition of life itself. Then you will know what landscape architecture is.

JENS JENSEN
QUOTED IN *THE STORY OF THE CLEARING* (1972)
MARTHA FULKERSON AND ADA CORSON

Grottoes. Islands of floating stone. Artificial mountains. Dwarf Trees in the form of pagodas and animals. Crags of marble and fountains of fantastic design. Strange Flowers. Houses of pleasure and relaxation.

JEAN CLAUDE PHILIPPE ISIDORE HEDDE
ON THE GARDENS OF SUZHOU
DÉSCRIPTION MÉTHODIQUE DES PRODUITS DIVERS RECUEILLIS DANS UN VOYAGE EN CHINE (1848)

Take thy plastic spade,
It is thy pencil; take thy seeds, thy plants,
They are thy colours.

WILLIAM MASON
THE ENGLISH GARDEN (1782)

Underlying all the greatest gardens are certain principles of composition which remain unchanged because they are rooted in the natural laws of the universe.

SYLVIA CROWE
GARDEN DESIGN (1959)

In a word he disdains to have a garden less than Pennsylvania and every den is an arbor, every run of water, a canal, and every small level spot a parterre, where he nurses up some of his idol flowers and cultivates his darling productions.

ALEXANDER GARDEN ON JOHN BARTRAM
LETTER TO CADWALLADER COLDEN, NOVEMBER 4, 1754
QUOTED IN *THE NATURES OF JOHN AND WILLIAM BARTRAM* (1996)
THOMAS P. SLAUGHTER

5

Branch and Blade

It may strike some readers as odd to combine quotes on trees and lawns in a single section, but it makes sense to me if only because they represent virtual opposites. Trees and grass are, respectively, the largest and smallest plants in the garden. Their requirements are also contrary. Once it is comfortably installed, a tree calls for almost no work on the part of the gardener, while most lawns exact an unconscionable amount of time and attention. In one way, of course, they are the same—a good garden needs both.

I have always had a strong affection for trees. The small town where I grew up, in Michigan, had streets lined with giant elms—now gone, alas—and the first nickel I ever earned came from hawking clusters of orange mountain-ash berries around the neighborhood, from a tree in our backyard. Trees were for climbing, building tree houses in, swinging on, stealing apples and plums from. Each piece of property I've ever owned came equipped with fine trees—indeed that may be what attracted me to them in the first place. Hemlocks, white pines, and maples in the Berkshires; oaks, beeches, ash, and a magnificent walnut in the marches of Wales; and on both sides of the Atlantic any number of old apple trees. Riches indeed.

With lawns my relationship has been more checkered. To begin with, they were mainly a source of income from mowing. I never reached the point of repugnance ambiguously announced by William Empson in his poem "Rolling the Lawn" ("Our final hope / Is flat despair"), but shoving a rusty push-mower for ten cents an hour couldn't be classed as a pleasure. These days, mechanized, I'm perfectly happy spending a couple of hours shearing what somebody has called my bumpysward. I almost (but not quite) resent giving up the job to the young man down the lane willing to do it for a tenner.

Some of my favorite quotes are in this section. Henry Mitchell is as usual precise and acerb in pinpointing the American tendency toward tree worship (*mea culpa*), while despite Katharine White's paean to the "special delights" of mown grass there's no getting around the truth of Michael Pollan's observation that a lawn is "nature under totalitarian rule." On an entirely different level is George Peele's mysteriously joyful discovery of God in "a pleasant wind"—I commend it to you.

Returning after the war had blown over, he caught the same disease that was killing the chestnut trees in those years, and passed away. It was the only case in history where a tree doctor had to be called in to spray a person, and our family felt it very keenly.

JAMES THURBER
"THE CAR WE HAD TO PUSH"
MY LIFE AND HARD TIMES (1933)

There appears to be a large element of tree worship in us Americans, and anything remotely connected with a tree is approached with a numinous awe. People who are slothful by nature and who never get around to cutting down the peony and lily stalks in November (though this is well worth the labor) and who never divide the irises on time, or plant the daffodil bulbs before Thanksgiving, or prune the climbing roses—such persons nevertheless leap into action when leaves fall, as if the fate of the garden depended on raking them immediately. I do not intend to comment on that situation, on the grounds that fiddling with leaves is no more harmful than cocktail parties, marijuana, stock car racing, and other little bees people get in their bonnets.

HENRY MITCHELL
THE ESSENTIAL EARTHMAN (1981)

A grass-blade's no easier to make than an oak.

JAMES RUSSELL LOWELL (1819–1891)

Trees growing—right in front of my window;
The trees are high and the leaves grow thick.
Sad alas! The distant mountain view
Obscured by this, dimly shows between.
One morning I took knife and axe;
With my own hand I lopped the branches off.
Ten thousand leaves fall about my head;
A thousand hills come before my eyes.
Suddenly, as when clouds or mists break
And straight through, the blue sky appears;
Again, like the face of a friend one has loved
Seen at last after an age of parting.
First there came a gentle wind blowing;
One by one the birds flew back to the tree.
To ease my mind I gazed to the South East;
As my eyes wandered, my thoughts went far away.

Of men there is none that has not some preference;
Of things there is none but mixes good with ill.
It was not that I did not love the tender branches;
But better still,—to see the green hills!

Po Chü-i (772–846)
"Pruning Trees"
A Hundred and Seventy Chinese Poems (1919)
Translated by Arthur Waley

Go forwarde in the name of God, graffe, set, plant, and nourishe
up trees in every corner of your grounde.

John Gerard
Herball or Generall Historie of Plantes (1597)

Transplanting trees is agitating work. Recollecting the dislocation
and distress a human can feel at being transplanted into a new
scene, one cannot help worrying when one moves a tree.

Clare Leighton
Four Hedges (1935)

God in the whizzing of a pleasant wind
Shall march upon the tops of mulberry trees.

GEORGE PEELE
DAVID AND FAIR BATHSABE (1599)

What right have we to deform things so lovely in form? No cramming of Chinese feet into impossible shoes is half so foolish as the wilful and brutal distortion of the beautiful forms of trees.

WILLIAM ROBINSON
ON TOPIARY
THE ENGLISH FLOWER GARDEN (1883)

Trees display the effects of breeding quite as much as horses, dogs, or men.

WILLIAM HOWITT
VISITS TO REMARKABLE PLACES (1842)

Trees are much like human beings and enjoy each other's company. Only a few love to be alone.

JENS JENSEN
SIFTINGS (1939)

I took money and bought flowering trees
And planted them out on the bank to the east of the Keep.
I simply bought whatever had the most blooms,
Not caring whether peach, apricot, or plum.
A hundred fruits, all mixed up together;
A thousand branches, flowering in due rotation.
Each has its season coming early or late;
But to all alike the fertile soil is kind.
The red flowers hang like a heavy mist;
The white flowers gleam like a fall of snow.

Po Chü-i (772–846)
"Planting Flowers by the Eastern Embankment"
A Hundred and Seventy Chinese Poems (1919)
Translated by Arthur Waley

While trees are excellent for apes, owls, and arboreal fauna in general, they are annoying in a small garden where one hopes to something besides a compost pile and a continental championship collection of slugs and sowbugs.

Henry Mitchell (1923–1993)

I like trees because they seem more resigned to the way they have to live than other things do.

WILLA CATHER (1876–1947)

Of all the wonders of nature, a tree in summer is perhaps the most remarkable; with the possible exception of a moose singing "Embraceable You" in spats.

WOODY ALLEN (1935–)

Great trees are good for nothing but shade.

GEORGE HERBERT
OUTLANDISH PROVERBS (1640)

He that plants trees loves others besides himself.

THOMAS FULLER
GNOMOLOGIA (1732)

Except during the nine months before he draws breath, no man manages his affairs as well as a tree does.

GEORGE BERNARD SHAW
MAXIMS FOR REVOLUTIONISTS (1906)

The nonagenarian President of Magdalen, Dr. Routh, was once brought the news that the acacia tree outside his lodgings had been blown down by a storm. "Put it up again," was all he said: and up, of course, it went.

JAMES MORRIS
OXFORD (1965)

Orchards are even more personal in their charms than gardens, as they are more nearly human creations.

AMOS BRONSON ALCOTT
TABLETS (1868)

At midday I reached my long-wished pinus . . . New or strange things seldom fail to make great impressions, and often at first we are liable to over-rate them; and lest I should never see my friends to tell them verbally of this most beautiful and immensely large tree, I now state the dimensions of the largest one I could find that was blown down by the wind: Three feet from the ground, 57 ft 9 in. in circumference; 134 feet from the ground, 17 ft 5 in.; extreme length, 215 feet.

DAVID DOUGLAS
ON THE DOUGLAS FIR (OREGON PINE)
JOURNAL, OCTOBER 26, 1826

Mallus the Appyll tree is a tree that berith apples: and is a grete tree in itself: But it is lesse and more shorte than other trees of the wood with knottes and ryveled rynde: and maketh shadowe with thycke bowes and braunches: fayre with divers blossomes and flores of sweetness & lykynge: with gode frute & noble. And is gracyous in sighte and in taste: and vertuous in medicyne . . .

BARTHOLOMAEUS ANGLICUS
DE PROPRIETATIBUS RERUM (THIRTEENTH CENTURY)
TRANSLATED BY JOHN OF TREVISA (1398, PUBLISHED 1495)

There is enough misery in the world without thinking of Norway maples.

HENRY MITCHELL
THE ESSENTIAL EARTHMAN (1981)

Loveliest of trees, the cherry now
Is hung with bloom along the bough.

A. E. HOUSMAN
A SHROPSHIRE LAD (1896)

You cannot imagine what a nice walk we had round the orchard . . . I hear today that an apricot has been detected on one of the trees.

JANE AUSTEN
LETTER, MAY 1808
JANE AUSTEN, HER LIFE AND LETTERS (1913)

I shall say absolutely nothing about the spindle tree.

SEI SHŌNAGON
THE PILLOW BOOK OF SEI SHŌNAGON (TENTH CENTURY)
TRANSLATED BY IVAN MORRIS (1967)

I always thought ill of people at home, who trimmed their shrubbery into pyramids, and squares, and spires, and all manner of unnatural shapes, and when I saw the same thing being practiced in this great park [of Versailles] I began to feel dissatisfied. But I soon saw the idea of the thing and the wisdom of it. They seek the *general* effect. We distort a dozen sickly trees into unaccustomed shapes in a little yard no bigger than a dining room, and then surely they look absurd enough. But here . . . they make trees take fifty different shapes . . . I will leave it to others to determine how these people manage to make endless ranks of lofty forest trees grow to just a certain thickness of trunk (say a foot and two-thirds); how they make them spring to precisely the same height for miles; how they make them grow so close together; how they compel one huge limb to spring from the same identical spot on each tree and form the main sweep of the arch; and how all these things are kept in exactly the same condition, and in the same exquisite shapeliness and symmetry month after month and year after year—for I have tried to reason out the problem, and have failed.

MARK TWAIN
THE INNOCENTS ABROAD (1869)

With honeysuckle, over-sweet, festooned;
With bitter ivy bound;
Terraced with funguses unsound;
Deformed with many a boss
And closéd scar, o'ercushioned deep with moss;
Bundled all about with pagan mistletoe;
And thick with nests of the hoarse bird
That talks, but understands not his own word;
Stands, and so stood a thousand years ago,
A single tree.

COVENTRY PATMORE
"ARBOR VITAE"
POEMS (1878)

A lawn is nature under totalitarian rule.

MICHAEL POLLAN
SECOND NATURE (1991)

The world is very flat—
There is no doubt of that.

E. V. RIEU
"NIGHT THOUGHT OF A TORTOISE SUFFERING FROM INSOMNIA ON A LAWN"
A PUFFIN QUARTET OF POETS (1958)

You can't beat English lawns. Our final hope
Is flat despair. Each morning ere
I greet the office, through the weekday air,
Holding the Holy Roller at the slope
(The English fetish, not the Texas Pope)
Hither and thither on my toes with care
I roll ours flatter and flatter. Long, in prayer
I grub for daisies at whose roots I grope.

WILLIAM EMPSON
"ROLLING THE LAWN"
COLLECTED POEMS OF WILLIAM EMPSON (1949)

Consider the many special delights a lawn affords: soft mattress
for a creeping baby; worm hatchery for a robin; croquet or
badminton court; baseball diamond; restful green perspectives
leading the eye to a background of flower border, shrubs, or hedge;
green shadows—"this lawn, a carpet all alive / With shadows flung
from leaves"—as changing and spellbinding as the waves of the
sea, whether flecked with sunlight under trees of light foliage,
like elm and locust, or deep, solid shade, moving slowly as the
tide, under maple and oak. This carpet! What pleasanter surface
on which to walk, sit, lie, or even to read Tennyson?

KATHARINE S. WHITE
ONWARD AND UPWARD IN THE GARDEN (1979)

Although the previous owner of the house had assured them that grass would not grow in the garden, Teinosuke was determined to have a try. He did indeed succeed in producing a lawn, but it was a very sickly lawn, always late to turn green in the spring. He worked twice as hard over it as most men would have. Discovering that the feebleness of the grass was owing at least in part to the fact that sparrows ate the early shoots, he worked almost full time each spring stoning sparrows. The rest of the family must help him, he insisted, and as the season approached they would say: "The time for the throwing of stones has come."

JUNICHIRO TANIZAKI
THE MAKIOKA SISTERS (1943–1948)
TRANSLATED BY E. G. SEIDENSTICKER (1957)

Mowing the grass once a fortnight in pleasure grounds, as now practised, is a costly mistake.

WILLIAM ROBINSON
THE WILD GARDEN (1870)

Nothing is more pleasant to the eye than green grass kept finely shorn.

FRANCIS BACON
OF GARDENS (1625)

I am not a lover of lawns. Rather would I see daisies in their thousands, ground ivy, hawkweed, and even the hated plantain with tall stems, and dandelions with splendid flowers and fairy down, than the too-well-tended lawn.

W. H. HUDSON
THE BOOK OF A NATURALIST (1919)

What gives it power makes it change its mind
At each extreme, and lean its rising rain
Down low, first one and then the other way;
In which exchange humility and pride
Reverse, forgive, arise, and then die again,
Wherefore it holds at both ends of the day
The rainbow in its scattering grains of spray.

HOWARD NEMEROV
"THE BEAUTIFUL LAWN SPRINKLER"
COLLECTED POEMS OF HOWARD NEMEROV (1977)

Grass is hard and lumpy and damp, and full of dreadful black insects.

OSCAR WILDE
THE DECAY OF LYING (1891)

Forests decay, harvests perish, flowers vanish, but grass is immortal.

JOHN J. INGALLS
SPEECH IN THE UNITED STATES SENATE (1874)

A blade of grass is always a blade of grass, whether in one country or another.

HESTER LYNCH PIOZZI
QUOTING SAMUEL JOHNSON
ANECDOTES OF THE LATE SAMUEL JOHNSON (1786)

Jack used to curse the front lawn as if it were a living thing
. . . [He] hated the front yard because he thought it was against
him. There had been a beautiful lawn there when Jack came along,
but he let it wander off into nothing. He refused to water it or
take care of it in any way.

Now the ground was so hard it gave his car flat tires in the
summer. The yard was always finding a nail to put into one of
his tires or the car was always sinking out of sight in the winter
when the rains came on.

RICHARD BRAUTIGAN
THE REVENGE OF THE LAWN (1971)

My men like satyrs grazing on the lawn
Shall with their goat-feet dance an antic hay.

CHRISTOPHER MARLOWE
EDWARD II (1594)

6

Observations

Next to gardening itself, one of the greatest joys of the sport (hobby, art—you name it) is visiting other people's gardens. Much garden-writing consists of describing the beauties to be found there, usually smothered in a blanket of adjectives. I have tried to stay away from such descriptive passages, largely because they generally lack the edge needed to convey an accurate sense of either the garden or the writer. But a few were irresistible. Among these are several translated from Japanese, profoundly scented with nostalgia, and some luscious accounts by such descriptive geniuses as Horace Walpole, William Beckford, and Colette. See a garden through their eyes and all is fresh again.

But it is the shorter, more pungent observations—sometimes on particular garden or aspect of gardening, sometimes on the very nature of gardening as an art—that make up the bulk of this section. Here is the very essence of the garden-writer as phrase-maker or epigrammatist. Smashed clichés, startlingly original thoughts, brave use of words (am I alone in feeling the hair on the back of my neck stand up when I hear Gerard Manley Hopkins speaking of "burning aspiration upon aspiration of scarlet geraniums"?)—all are represented here, along with such delightful confessions as that of the artist Henry Holman Hunt: "I feel really frightened when I sit down to paint a flower."

I trust that no one will object to one other inclusion that no book of garden quotes should be without: the seduction scene, set in a garden, from *Pickwick Papers*. I am especially fond of the happy watering pot.

Under that heat haze the great garden lived like a happy beast, released from the world, far from everything, freed from everything.

EMILE ZOLA
LA FAUTE DE L'ABBE MOURET (1875)

It is a marvel what children, dogs, plants, and baby birds can pack into their insides without coming to any apparent harm.

H. L. V. FLETCHER
PUREST PLEASURE (1949)

A U garden need not be large. Herbaceous borders are U, and so are weeds. Neat beds of annuals and yellow conifers, especially the dwarf species, are non-U. But yew is always U.

ROBIN BRACKENBURY
WHAT ARE U? (1969)
EDITED BY ALAN S. C. ROSS

The cherries in the Heian Shrine were left to the last because they, of all the cherries in Kyoto, were the most beautiful. Now that the great weeping cherry in Gion was dying and its blossoms were growing paler each year, what was left to stand for the Kyoto spring if not the cherries in the Heian Shrine? And so, coming back from the western suburbs on the afternoon of the second day, and picking that moment of regret when the spring sun was about to set, they would pause, a little tired, under the trailing branches, and look fondly at each tree—on around the lake, by the approach to a bridge, by a bend in the path, under the eaves of the gallery. And, until the cherries came the following year, they could close their eyes and see again the color and line of a trailing branch.

JUNICHIRO TANIZAKI
THE MAKIOKA SISTERS (1943–1948)
TRANSLATED BY E. G. SEIDENSTICKER (1957)

You ask about the house and garden. There is not much garden, and the soil is sandy, but we are getting somewhere at last . . . We have three beautiful mature gum trees, the only things growing here when we came, and we have planted roses, several special hibiscus, and a number of native things. Azaleas are our great standby. They are so wiry, and stand up to the gales which sweep us. At the back, which is full of statuesque cats and pregnant pugs, we have a "Greek" Terrace on top of two garages—

that is, vines growing over a pergola, and lots of pots with geraniums, herbs etc. There is also an ugly but necessary clothes line, a patch of grass for the dogs to do their business on, more hibiscus, frangipani (which I don't much care for—too much like Hanualulu and Flahrida) and a flourishing lemon tree. The general effect and the vibrations are right.

PATRICK WHITE
LETTER TO JAMES STERN, MARCH 20, 1966
PATRICK WHITE LETTERS (1994)
EDITED BY DAVID MARR

Gardening is . . . an outlet for fanaticism, violence, love, and rationality without their worst side effects.

GEOFFREY CHARLESWORTH
A GARDENER OBSESSED (1994)

Strawberry Hill, June 10, 1765. Eleven at night. I am just come out of the garden in the most oriental of all evenings, and from breathing odours beyond those of Araby. The acacias, which the Arabians have the sense to worship, are covered with blossoms, the honeysuckles dangle from every tree in festoons, the seringas are thickets of sweets, and the new-cut hay in the field tempers the balmy gales with simple freshness; while a thousand sky-rockets launched into the air at Ranelagh or Marybone illuminate the scene, and give it an air of Haroun Alraschid's paradise.

HORACE WALPOLE
THE LETTERS OF HORACE WALPOLE (1926)
EDITED BY WILLIAM HADLEY

How fair is a garden amid the trials and passions of existence.

BENJAMIN DISRAELI (1804–1881)

What is all this juice and all this joy?
A strain of earth's sweet being in the beginning
In Eden garden.

GERARD MANLEY HOPKINS
"SPRING"
POEMS (1918)

"That was the best garden," he said, "which produced the most roots and fruits; and that water was most to be prized which contained the most fish."

HESTER LYNCH PIOZZI
QUOTING SAMUEL JOHNSON
ANECDOTES OF THE LATE SAMUEL JOHNSON (1786)

There is no virtue which I do not attribute to the man who loves to project and execute gardening.

CHARLES JOSEPH, PRINCE DE LIGNE
COUP D'ŒIL SUR BELŒIL (1781)

It hedged was with honeysuckles,
Or periclimenum;
Well mixed with small cornus trees,
Sweet briar and ligustrum.
The white thorn, and the blackthorn both
With box and maple fine:
In which branched the briony
The ivy and the wild vine.

JOHN HALL
POEMS (1646)

True Brahmin, in the morning meadows wet,
    Expound the Vedas on the violet,
Or, hid in vines, peeping through many a loop,
    See the plum redden, and the beurré stoop.

RALPH WALDO EMERSON (1803–1882)

Gardening is certainly the next amusement to reading; and as my sight will now permit me little of that, I am glad to form a taste that can give me so much employment.

LADY MARY WORTLEY MONTAGU (1689–1762)
LETTER TO HER DAUGHTER
COMPLETE LETTERS (1965–1966)
EDITED BY R. HALSBAND

[My Mother] could snatch a dry root from field or hedgerow, dab it into the garden, give it a shake—and almost immediately it flowered. One felt she could grow roses from a stick or a chair-leg, so remarkable was this gift.

LAURIE LEE
CIDER WITH ROSIE (1959)

In a marshy spot in the garden we had excavated a pit, forming a pond, around which stood a grove of pine trees. It looks as if, in five or six years, a thousand years have left their mark here— one bank of the pond has collapsed, new trees have sprung up among the old, and such is the general air of neglect that all

who look are afflicted with a sense of sadness. Old memories
come flooding back . . .

Ki no Tsurayuki
The Tosa Diary (CA. 936)
Translated by G. W. Sargent
Anthology of Japanese Literature (1955)
Edited by Donald Keene

Rome, 30th June 1782. As soon as the sun declined I strolled
into the Villa Medici; but finding it haunted by pompous people,
nay, even by the Spanish Ambassador, and several red-legged
Cardinals, I moved off to the Negroni garden. There I found
what my soul desired, thickets of jasmine, and wild spots
overgrown with bay; long alleys of cypress totally neglected, and
almost impassable through the luxuriance of the vegetation; on
every side antique fragments, vases, sarcophagi, and altars sacred
to the Manes, in deep, shady recesses, which I am certain the
Manes must love. The air was filled with the murmurs of water,
trickling down basins of porphyry, and losing itself amongst
overgrown weeds and grasses.

William Beckford
Italy; with Sketches of Spain and Portugal (1834)

On summer Saturday evenings we walked round the garden between dances, feeling unlike ourselves. The garden was long, with lime trees and apple trees and long grass with cuckoo flowers in it: it looked very beautiful in the late evening light, with the sound of the piano coming out through the gymnasium door.

ELIZABETH BOWEN
THE MULBERRY TREE (1986)

Remains of you in this grass
We once used to tread;
How long ago it was we came—
Nothing whatsoever—
The garden now is a wilderness.

FUJIWARA NO YASUSUE (TWELFTH CENTURY)
FROM *SHINKOKINSHŪ*
TRANSLATED BY DONALD KEENE
ANTHOLOGY OF JAPANESE LITERATURE (1955)
EDITED BY DONALD KEENE

I possessed my soul and finally, though the delay was long, perceived some appearances of bloom.

HENRY JAMES
THE ASPERN PAPERS (1888)

Is it worth while, I wonder, seeking for adequate words to describe the rest? I shall never be able to conjure up the splendor that adorns, in my memory, the ruddy festoons of an autumn vine borne down by its own weight and clinging despairingly to some branch of the fir-trees. And the massive lilacs, whose compact flowers—blue in the shade and purple in the sunshine— withered so soon, stifled by their own exuberance. The lilacs long since dead will not be revived at my bidding, any more than the terrifying moonlight—silver, quick-silver, leaden-grey, with facets of dazzling amethyst or scintillating points of sapphire—all depending on a certain pane in the blue glass window of the summer-house at the bottom of the garden.

COLETTE
MY MOTHER'S HOUSE (1922)

"Faced with the alternatives of giving up my botanical expeditions and being obliged to call upon a degrading person, I chose the former calamity. Besides, when it comes to that, there was no need to go quite so far. It seems that here, in my own little bit of garden, more odd things happen in broad daylight than at midnight—in the Bois de Boulogne! Only they attract no attention, because among flowers it's all done quite simply, you see an orange shower, or else a very dusty fly coming to wipe its feet or take a bath before crawling into a flower. And that does the trick!" "The cabinet the plant is standing on is splendid too; it's Empire, I think," said the Princess, who, not being familiar with the works of Darwin and his followers, was unable to grasp the point of the Duchess's pleasantries.

MARCEL PROUST
REMEMBRANCE OF THINGS PAST (THE GUERMANTES WAY, 1920*)*
TRANSLATED BY C. K. SCOTT MONCRIEFF (1925)

Indeed, it is the Purest of Human pleasures. It is the greatest Refreshment to the Spirit of Man; Without which, Buildings and Pallaces are but Grosse Handy-Works: And a Man shall ever see, that when Ages grow to Civility and Elegancie, Men come to build Stately, sooner then to Garden finely: As if Gardening were the greater Perfection.

FRANCIS BACON
OF GARDENS (1625)

Before the flowers open I often look to see if they are
    yet open
And when they begin to open I fear that wind and rain may
    come.
After the flowers have opened I care not for wind and rain;
I only care if you come not, to drink deep beneath the
    flowers.

LIU YIN (1249–1293)
"TO MAGNOLIA FLOWERS"
THE PENGUIN BOOK OF CHINESE VERSE (1962)
TRANSLATED BY ROBERT KOTEWALL AND NORMAN L. SMITH

The garden is all heights, terraces, Excelsiors, misty mountain tops, seats up trees called Crows' Nests, flights of steps seemingly up to heaven lined with burning aspiration upon aspiration of scarlet geraniums.

GERARD MANLEY HOPKINS
LETTER, 1874
FURTHER LETTERS OF GERARD MANLEY HOPKINS (1938)
EDITED BY CLAUDE COLLEER ABBOTT

It would be unreasonable to demand that anything as lovely as an herbaceous border in full bloom be achieved without a little suffering.

ELEANOR PERÉNYI
GREEN THOUGHTS (1981)

It will be long, I hope, before Ridings, Parks, Pleasure Grounds, Gardens, and ornamented farms grow so much in fashion in America. But Nature has done greater things and furnished nobler materials there. The oceans, islands, rivers, mountains, valleys, are all laid out upon a larger scale.

JOHN ADAMS (1787?)
QUOTED IN *AMERICAN GARDENS OF THE NINETEENTH CENTURY* (1987)
ANN LEIGHTON

Some American will . . . revive the true taste in gardening . . . I love to skip into futurity and imagine what will be done on the giant scale of a new hemisphere.

HORACE WALPOLE
QUOTED IN *OBSERVATIONS, ANECDOTES, AND CHARACTERS OF BOOKS AND MEN* (1820)
JOSEPH SPENCE

Let no one visit America without having first studied botany; it is an amusement, as a clever friend of mine once told me, that helps one wonderfully up and down hill, and must be superlatively valuable in America, both from the plentiful lack of other amusements, and the plentiful material for enjoyment in this; besides, if one is dying to know the name of any of these lovely strangers, it is a thousand to one against his finding anyone who can tell it.

FRANCES TROLLOPE
DOMESTIC MANNERS OF THE AMERICANS (1832)

But though an old man, I am but a young gardener.

THOMAS JEFFERSON
LETTER TO CHARLES WILLSON PEALE, AUGUST 20, 1811
THOMAS JEFFERSON'S GARDEN BOOK (1944)
EDITED BY E. M. BETTS

Who would not joy to see his conquering hand
Oe'r all the vegetable world command?
And the wild gyants of the wood receive
 What law hee's pleas'd to give?

ABRAHAM COWLEY
THE GARDEN (1666)

It seems to me far from an exaggeration that good professors are not more essential to a college, than a spacious garden, which ought to be formed with the nicest elegance, tempered with simplicity, rejecting sumptuous and glaring ornaments.

HENRY HOME, LORD KAMES
ELEMENTS OF CRITICISM (1762)

The man who has planted a garden feels that he has done something for the good of the world.

CHARLES DUDLEY WARNER
MY SUMMER IN A GARDEN (1871)

"There's never a garden in all the parish but what there's endless waste in it for want o' somebody could use everything up . . . It sets one thinking, that—gardening does."

GEORGE ELIOT
SILAS MARNER (1861)

Flowers are the sweetest things God ever made, and forgot to put a soul into.

HENRY BEECHER
LIFE THOUGHTS (1858)

I feel really frightened when I sit down to paint a flower.

HENRY HOLMAN HUNT (1827–1910)

———

"I have forgotten my flowers," said the spinster aunt.

"Water them now," said Mr. Tupman, in accents of persuasion.

"You will take cold in the evening air," urged the spinster aunt, affectionately.

"No, no," said Mr. Tupman, rising; "it will do me good. Let me accompany you."

The lady paused to adjust the sling in which the left arm of the youth was placed, and taking his right arm led him to the garden.

There was a bower to the further end, with honeysuckle, jessamine, and creeping plants—one of those sweet retreats which humane men erect for the accomodation of spiders.

The spinster aunt took up a large watering pot which lay in one corner, and was about to leave the arbor. Mr. Tupman detained her, and drew her to a seat beside him.

"Miss Wardle!" said he.

The spinster aunt trembled, till some pebbles which had accidentally found their way into the large watering pot shook like an infant's rattle.

"Miss Wardle," said Mr. Tupman, "you are an angel."

"Mr. Tupman!" exclaimed Rachael, blushing as red as the watering pot itself.

"Nay," said the eloquent Pickwickian—"I know it but too well."

"All women are angels, they say," murmured the lady, playfully.

"Then what can *you* be; or to what, without presumption, can I compare you?" replied Mr. Tupman. "Where was the woman ever seen, who resembled you? Where else could I seek to—Oh!" Here Mr. Tupman paused, and pressed the hand which clasped the handle of the happy watering pot.

CHARLES DICKENS
THE POSTHUMOUS PAPERS OF THE PICKWICK CLUB (1837)

[My garden] is a confusion of kitchen and parterre, orchard and flower garden, which lie so mixt and interwoven with one another, that if a foreigner, who had seen nothing of our country, should be conveyed into my garden at his first landing, he would look upon it as a natural wilderness, and one of the uncultivated parts of our country.

JOSEPH ADDISON
THE TATLER (1710)

It is proper to hate the marks of shoes on the green
    moss;
Of ten that knock at this brushwood gate, nine cannot
    have it opened.
Spring colours fill the garden but cannot all be
    contained,
For one spray of red almond-blossom peeps out from the
    wall.

YEH SHAO-WENG (LATE TWELFTH TO EARLY THIRTEENTH CENTURY)
"ON VISITING A GARDEN WHEN ITS MASTER IS ABSENT"
THE PENGUIN BOOK OF CHINESE VERSE (1962)
TRANSLATED BY ROBERT KOTEWALL AND NORMAN L. SMITH

Perhaps our best hope for gardening as an art is that gardening
is an activity whose never-achieved aim is progress towards a
never-completed work of art.

GEOFFREY CHARLESWORTH
THE OPINIONATED GARDENER (1988)

The force that through the green fuse drives the flower
Drives my green age.

DYLAN THOMAS
"THE FORCE THAT THROUGH THE GREEN FUSE DRIVES THE FLOWER"
COLLECTED POEMS (1952)

There has been a class of men whose patriotic affection, or whose general benevolence, has been usually defrauded of the gratitude their country owes them: these have been the introducers of new flowers, new plants, and new roots.

ISAAC D'ISRAELI
CURIOSITIES OF LITERATURE (1834)

I had not the smallest taste for growing [plants], or taking care of them. My whole time passed in staring at them, or into them. In no morbid curiosity, but in admiring wonder, I pulled every flower to pieces till I knew all that could be seen of it with a child's eyes.

JOHN RUSKIN
PRAETERITA (1885)

I think it funny how our rubbish dump has blundered into fame.

V. SACKVILLE-WEST
ON SISSINGHURST
LETTER TO HAROLD NICOLSON, SEPTEMBER 29, 1954
QUOTED IN *VITA'S OTHER WORLD* (1985)
JANE BROWN

Doctor Hackwill in his Apology for the world's not decaying, tells a story of a German gentleman who lived fourteen yeares without receiving any nourishment downe his throat, but onely walked in a spacious Garden full of Odoriferous Herbes and Flowers.

WILLIAM COLES
THE ART OF SIMPLING (1656)

Who would look dangerously up at Planets that might safely look downe at Plants?

JOHN GERARD
HERBALL OR GENERALL HISTORIE OF PLANTES (1597)

Half the interest of a garden is the constant exercise of the imagination.

MRS. C. W. EARLE
POT-POURRI FROM A SURREY GARDEN (1897)

No poet I've ever heard of has written an ode to a load of manure.

RUTH STOUT
HOW TO HAVE A GREEN THUMB WITHOUT AN ACHING BACK (1955)

There is not a sprig of grass that shoots uninteresting to me.

THOMAS JEFFERSON
LETTER TO MARTHA JEFFERSON RANDALL, 1790
THOMAS JEFFERSON'S GARDEN BOOK (1944)
EDITED BY E. M. BETTS

Little by little, even with other cares, the slowly but surely working poison of the garden-mania begins to stir in my long-sluggish veins.

HENRY JAMES (1843–1916)

A doctor can bury his mistakes but an architect can only advise his client to plant vines.

FRANK LLOYD WRIGHT (1869–1959)

I appreciate the misunderstanding I have had with Nature over my perennial border. I think it is a flower garden; she thinks it is a meadow lacking grass, and tries to correct the error.

SARA STEIN
MY WEEDS (1988)

I could go on and on. But that is just what gardening is, going on and on.

MARGERY FISH
WE MADE A GARDEN (1956)

'Tis my faith that every flower
Enjoys the air it breathes!

WILLIAM WORDSWORTH
"LINES WRITTEN IN EARLY SPRING"
LYRICAL BALLADS (1798)

I am not fond of the idea of my shrubberies being always approachable.

JANE AUSTEN
PERSUASION (1818)

The garden is in a pitiful state with all the bamboo and lattice fences knocked over and lying next to each other on the ground. It is bad enough that the branches of one of the great trees have been broken by the wind; but it is a really painful surprise to find that the tree itself has fallen down and is now lying flat over the bush-clover and the valerians. As one sits in one's room looking out, the wind, as though on purpose, gently blows the leaves one by one through the chinks of the lattice-window.

SEI SHŌNAGON
THE PILLOW BOOK OF SEI SHŌNAGON (TENTH CENTURY)
TRANSLATED BY IVAN MORRIS (1967)

Psychoanalysis on the basis of one's scree or woodland is out of place. But you can't help thinking that there must be something written there, if only you knew how to read it.

GEOFFREY CHARLESWORTH
THE OPINIONATED GARDENER (1988)

I am become a great florist, and shrub-doctor.

WILLIAM COWPER
LETTER TO HIS COUSIN FRANCES COWPER, MARCH 14, 1767
SELECTED LETTERS (1926)
EDITED BY W. HADLEY

The form of the orange-tree, the cocoa-nut, the mango, the tree-fern, the banana, will remain clear and separate; but the thousand beauties which unite these into one perfect scene must fade away; yet they will leave, like a tale told in childhood, a picture full of indistinct, but most beautiful figures.

CHARLES DARWIN
THE VOYAGE OF THE BEAGLE (1839)

Most poems about plants are even more indifferent to their natural properties than poems about animals.

W. H. AUDEN
A CERTAIN WORLD (1971)

Jaundice

Civilized they may be, but people who write about gardens can occasionally display a streak of savagery. I confess that it rather appeals to me. Jaundice is an agreeable antidote to the saccharine approach. Sometimes it arises from no more than a strong feeling about the way things are done (not *their* way), sometimes from a natural-born grumpiness, sometimes from what one hopes is a temporary disaffection with gardening and all its works. Whatever its origin, the result is some of the crispest and most memorable quotes I've run into yet.

A few of them, admittedly, are not by gardeners. Samuel Johnson, in fact, may be classed as an anti-gardener—he had no time for grottoes (fashionable in the eighteenth century) or much else to do with horticulture, though so far as I know he had no objection to eating vegetables. Thomas Fuller, whose delightfully vehement attack on the "Toolip" will live in infamy, is best known for his vast *History of the Worthies of England*; Charles Lamb referred to him as a "dear, fine, silly, old angel," and his horticultural exploits seem to have been limited to theorizing about the emblematic meaning of flowers. It is unlikely that either Shelley or the Duc de St. Simon ever laid a hand to a spade, but that did not stop them from making

151

sharp comments about the failings of other people's gardens—even, in St. Simon's case, gardens belonging to his own King Louis XIV.

Some might say that jaundice has no place in a garden, but that's like saying bad temper or strong opinions have no place in the world. There's never any shortage of people telling us how happy we ought to be there amidst our teucrium and our "Toolips." While I'd hate to be thought a spoilsport, maybe it's time for a little cynicism. Now and then, let's hear it for the curmudgeons.

"Yet, Sir, (said I) there are many people who are content to live in the country." JOHNSON. "Sir . . . they who are content to live in the country , are *fit* to live in the country."

JAMES BOSWELL
LIFE OF JOHNSON (1791)

It is pure unadulterated country life. They get up early because there is so much to do and go to bed early because they have so little to think about.

OSCAR WILDE (1854–1900)

Nature is the gardener's opponent. The gardener who pretends he is in love with her, has to destroy her climaxes of vegetation and make . . . an alliance with her which she will be the first to break without warning, in the most treasonable way she can. She sneaks in, she inserts her weeds, her couch-grass, her ground elder, her plantain, her greenfly and her slugs behind his back. The bitch.

GEOFFREY GRIGSON
GARDENAGE (1952)

Don't think I haven't tried; I have fertilized my crops with a variety of stimulants. I have scattered Hitler's speeches and most of DuPont's most expensive chemicals over their stunted growths, but so far all I have to show for my trouble is a small bed of wild marijuana, a sprig of mint, and a dislocation of the trunk muscles that has an excellent chance of developing into a full-blown rupture . . . I only hope that Uncle Sam isn't relying too heavily on my Victory Crop to sustain the nation through the coming winter.

GROUCHO MARX
GROUCHO MARX AND OTHER SHORT STORIES AND TALL TALES (1993)
EDITED BY ROBERT S. BADER

Lady Cantal says that flowers can feel no pain. I asked her if hers did, and she said yes, so I pointed to a hideous stone gnome overlooking a bed of very nice Stocks and told her the reason.

H. L. V. FLETCHER
PUREST PLEASURE (1949)

. . . I have to warn myself quickly against the anæmic approach of certain modern purists who have pushed the theory of understatement in planting to ridiculous lengths, planting one bulrush and one *Caltha palustris*, for example, in a formal pool in the patio of some elaborate modern house, or else thinking that a patch of marram grass and a few tufts of osier will enhance the bright *avant-garde* conceits of a pavilion at an exhibition. Such aridities, and they are increasingly frequent, are a bleak denial of all the pleasures of gardening.

RUSSELL PAGE
THE EDUCATION OF A GARDENER (1962)

Your African marigolds have just about as much freshness as the leather of a new football, without the quality of being easily kicked out of the way.

CHRISTOPHER LLOYD
THE WELL-TEMPERED GARDEN (1973)

His gardens next your admiration call:
On every side you look, behold the wall!
No pleasing intricacies intervene,
No artful wildness to perplex the scene;
Grove nods at grove, each alley has a brother,
And half the platform just reflects the other.

The suff'ring eye inverted nature sees,
Trees cut to statues, statues thick as trees;
With here a fountain never to be played;
And there a summerhouse that knows no shade;
Here Amphitrite sails through myrtle bowers;
There gladiators fight, or die in flowers;
Unwatered see the drooping sea-horse mourn
And swallows roost in Nilus' dusty urn.

ALEXANDER POPE
"OF THE USE OF RICHES"
EPISTLE TO BURLINGTON (1735)

Greenfly, it's difficult to see
Why God, who made the rose, made thee.

A. P. HERBERT
LOOK BACK AND LAUGH (1960)

You could hardly see any beautiful, pale, bright, yellow-green
of spring, every tree appeared to be entirely covered with a waving
mass of pink or mauve tissue paper. The daffodils were so thick
on the ground that they too obscured the green, they were new

varieties of terrifying size, either dead white or dark yellow, thick and fleshy; they did not look at all like the fragile friends of one's childhood. The whole effect was of a scene for musical comedy.

NANCY MITFORD
ON THE NON-U GARDEN OF SIR LEICESTER KROESIG
THE PURSUIT OF LOVE (1945)

I am a sundial, and I make a botch
Of what is done far better by a watch.

HILAIRE BELLOC
COMPLETE VERSE (1954)

I am a sundial. Ordinary words
Cannot express my thoughts on birds.

HILAIRE BELLOC
COMPLETE VERSE (1954)

Pessimistic moods, like caterpillars, feed on the gardener's happiness.

DEBORAH KELLAWAY
THE MAKING OF AN ENGLISH COUNTRY GARDEN (1988)

Evergloom of official titivation—
Uniform at the reservoir, and the chapel,
And the graveyard park,

Ugly as a brass-band in India.

TED HUGHES
"RHODODENDRONS"
NEW SELECTED POEMS 1957–1994 (1995)

There is lately a *Flower* (shal I call it so? in courtesie I will tearme it so, though it deserve not the appellation) a *Toolip*, which hath engrafted the love and affection of most people unto it; and what is this Toolip? a well-complexion'd stink, an ill favour wrapt up in pleasant colours.

THOMAS FULLER
ANTHEOLOGIA, OR THE SPEECH OF FLOWERS: PARTLY MORALL, PARTLY MISTICALL (1660)

Man was made for better things than pruning his rose trees.

COLIN WILSON
A BOOK OF GARDENS (1963)

Sunday, 23rd [January 1788]. I strolled to the gardens of the Buen Retiro, which contains neither statues nor fountains worth descrbing. They cover a vast extent of sandy ground, in which there is no prevailing upon anything vegetable or animal to survive, except ostriches, a troop of which were striding about in high spirits, apparently as much at home as in their own native parched-up deserts.

WILLIAM BECKFORD
ITALY; WITH SKETCHES OF SPAIN AND PORTUGAL (1834)

A garden is like those pernicious machineries which catch a man's coat-skirt or his hand, and draw in his arm, his leg, and his whole body to irresistible destruction.

RALPH WALDO EMERSON
THE CONDUCT OF LIFE (1860)

We saw the palace and garden of Versailles . . . full of statues, vases, fountains, and colonnades. In all that belongs essentially to a garden they are extraordinarily deficient.

PERCY BYSSHE SHELLEY
JOURNAL, SEPTEMBER 3, 1816

It is quite true that I have no great love for herbaceous borders or the plants that usually fill them—coarse things with no delicacy or quality about them. I think the only justification for such borders is that they shall be perfectly planned, both in regard to colour and to grouping; perfectly staked—and perfectly weeded.

V. SACKVILLE-WEST
VITA SACKVILLE-WEST'S GARDEN BOOK (1968)
EDITED BY PHILIPPA NICHOLSON

A garden is *not* a wild place—here is the great error of the extreme landscapists; therefore any attempt to make it so by incoherence and floppiness of line falls between two stools and is doubly damned, being neither real Nature nor real art.

REGINALD FARRER
MY ROCK-GARDEN (1920)

The Lincolnshire lady who shewed him a grotto she had been making came off no better . . . Would it not be a pretty cool habitation in summer? Said she, Mr Johnson? "I think it would, Madam (replied he)—for a toad."

HESTER LYNCH PIOZZI
ANECDOTES OF THE LATE SAMUEL JOHNSON (1786)

My garden will never make me famous
I'm a horticultural ignoramus.

OGDEN NASH (1902–1971)

Hedges, as such, are universally bad. They discover art in nature's province.

WILLIAM SHENSTONE
"UNCONNECTED THOUGHTS ON GARDENING"
THE WORKS IN PROSE AND VERSE OF WILLIAM SHENSTONE, ESQ. (1764)

Flowers in masses are mighty strong colour, and if not used with a great deal of caution are very destructive to pleasure in gardening . . . There are some flowers—inventions of men, *i.e.* florists—which are a bad colour altogether, and not to be used at all. Scarlet geraniums, for instance, or the yellow calceolaria, which, indeed, are not uncommonly grown together profusely, in order, I suppose, to show that even flowers can be thoroughly ugly.

WILLIAM MORRIS
HOPES AND FEARS FOR ART (1882)

The gardens, which are astonishingly magnificent, but discouraging to use, are in equally bad taste. One cannot reach the freshness of the shade without passing through a torrid zone, at the end of which one has no choice but to climb and then descend a small hill, and here the gardens end. The stone path burns one's feet, but without it, one sinks into the sand and into the blackest dirt. The violence done to nature everywhere disgusts; the abundant waters, forced up and collected again, are green, thick, muddy; they shed an unhealthy and perceptible humidity, a smell which is even worse. The whole effect, which one must yet treat with respect, is incomparable, but it is something to admire, and to shun.

Le Duc de Saint-Simon
on Versailles
Memoirs (the year 1680) (1829–1830)

The ornament whose merit soonest fades is the hermitage or scene adapted to contemplation. It is almost comic to set aside a quarter of one's garden to be melancholy in.

Horace Walpole
On Modern Gardening (1780)

Most of the People who sell the Trees and Plants in Stocks and other Markets are Fruiterers who understand no more of Gardening than a Gardener does of the making up of Compound Medicines of an Apothecary. They often tell us that the plants will prosper, when there is no Reason or Hopes for their growing at all; for I and others have seen Plants which were to be sold in the Markets, that were as uncertain of growth as a piece of Noah's Ark would be if we had it here to plant.

THOMAS FAIRCHILD
THE CITY GARDENER (1722)

Genesis got it just wrong. Adam should have been exiled from town as a punishment, and put to slave in a garden.

CLARENCE DAY
"HUMPTY-DUMPTY AND ADAM"
AFTER ALL (1936)

I can admire and enjoy most flowers, but just a few I positively dislike. Collarette Dahlias and those superlatively double African Marigolds that look like india-rubber bath sponges offend me most of all. I dislike the cheap thin texture of Godetias almost as much as I do the sinful magenta streaks and splotches that run in the blood of that family. I loathe Celosias equally with dyed Pampas grass; and Coxcombs, and spotty, marbled, double Balsams I should like to smash up with a coal-hammer; and certain great flaunting mauve and purple Cattleyas cloy my nose and annoy my eye till I conjure up a vision of them expiating their gaudy double-dyed wickedness with heads impaled on stiff wires like those of criminals on pikes, in a sea of *Asparagua Sprengeri*, and forming the bouquet presented to the wife of a provincial Mayor on the occasion of his opening the new sewerage works.

EDWARD AUGUSTUS BOWLES
MY GARDEN IN SUMMER (1914)

I have not yet seen any garden in Italy worth taking notice of.

JOSEPH ADDISON (1703)
WORKS (1856)
EDITED BY RICHARD HURD

The Italians understand, because they study, the excellencies of art; but they have no idea of the beauties of nature.

TOBIAS SMOLLETT
TRAVELS THROUGH FRANCE AND ITALY (1765)

I have come to understand the unspeakable loveliness of a solitary spray of blossoms arranged as only a Japanese expert knows how to arrange it . . . and therefore I cannot think now of what we Occidentals call a "bouquet" as anything but a vulgar murdering of flowers, an outrage upon the color-sense, a brutality, an abomination.

LAFCADIO HEARN
GLIMPSES OF UNFAMILIAR JAPAN (1894)

July 23 [1780].—We were driven in the evening to Nymphenburg, the Elector's country palace, the bosquets, jets d'eaux, and parterres of which are the pride of the Bavarians. The principal platform is all of a glitter with gilded Cupids and shining serpents spouting at every pore. Beds of poppies, hollyhocks, scarlet lychnis, and other flame-coloured flowers, border the edge of the walks, which extend till the perspective appears to meet and swarm with ladies and gentlemen in party-coloured raiment. The Queen of Golconda's gardens in a French opera are scarcely more gaudy and artificial. Unluckily too, the evening was fine, and the sun so powerful that we were half roasted before we could cross the great avenue and enter the thickets, which barely conceal very a splendid hermitage.

WILLIAM BECKFORD
ITALY; WITH SKETCHES OF SPAIN AND PORTUGAL (1834)

I'm afraid I can never be quite serious about a garden.

THE HON. MRS. E. V. BOYLE
DAYS AND HOURS IN A GARDEN (1884)

When Lord Teviot had despatched his letters, he found her in her garden ... [it was] a first-rate gardener's garden, every plant forming part of a group, and not to be picked or touched on any account; all of them forced into bloom at the wrong time of the year; and each bearing a name that it was difficult to pronounce, and impossible to remember.

EMILY EDEN
THE SEMI-ATTACHED COUPLE (1830)

Phloxes smell to me like a combination of pepper and pig-stye, most brooms of dirty, soapy bath-sponge, hawthorn of fish-shop, and meadow-sweet of curry powder.

EDWARD AUGUSTUS BOWLES
MY GARDEN IN SUMMER (1914)

In the plan of human conduct there is a marked difference between the mind which sees beauty in a simple violet and that which sees it in a pompous rose or dahlia. On the one hand we have a love for the free and untampered flowers of God's creation, and on the other hand for a flower of social ills, sophistication, and conceit.

JENS JENSEN
SIFTINGS (1939)

I recoil only from black plastic. Black plastic is not a mulch; it is an abomination.

SARA STEIN
MY WEEDS (1988)

The pleasure and Use of Gardens were unknown to our great Grandfathers: They were contented with Pot-herbs: and did mind chiefly their stables.

JOHN AUBREY (SEVENTEENTH CENTURY)
BRIEF LIVES (PUBLISHED 1813)

Of all ugly things, nothing is worse than the variegated conifer, which usually perishes as soon as its variegated parts die, the half dead tree often becoming a bush full of wisps of hay.

WILLIAM ROBINSON
THE ENGLISH FLOWER GARDEN (SIXTH EDITION, 1898)

Besides all this and spotted by awful white rocks and holed limestone rocks like a great fungus, there was the pink bluebell glade. Miss Anna Rose often remarked to him upon the prolific beauty of the pink bluebells which some aunt of hers had planted here. And he always refrained from expressing his absolute preference for blue bluebells. Only the very young prefer pink bluebells to blue. Equally, they prefer pink primroses to yellow.

MOLLY KEANE
TREASURE HUNT (1952)

I hate rose gardens. I never know why people have them—they don't have weigela gardens or philadelphus gardens.

SIR SIMON HORNBY, PRESIDENT OF THE ROYAL HORTICULTURAL SOCIETY
QUOTED IN *GARDENS ILLUSTRATED* (1993)

Marise's manner was faultless; she had asked: "How are your hollyhocks?" But not as if she had seen a hollyhock grow.

ELIZABETH BOWEN
FRIENDS AND RELATIONS (1931)

The blossom of the pear tree is the most prosaic, vulgar thing in the world. The less one sees of this particular blossom the better.

SEI SHŌNAGON
THE PILLOW BOOK OF SEI SHŌNAGON (TENTH CENTURY)
TRANSLATED BY IVAN MORRIS (1967)

If one indulges in extravagant earthmoving and planting, valuing colorful effects, then [a garden] becomes like a fetter, a mere cage.

WEN ZHENHENG
TREATISE ON SUPERFLUOUS THINGS (CA. 1615–1620)

To the man with brown fingers, a plant may just as well be inanimate, and by the time he is finished with it, it is.

CHRISTOPHER LLOYD
THE WELL-TEMPERED GARDEN (1985)

The hotbed swarmed with grubs; and in spite of the warm layers of dead leaves, under the painted frames and chalk-smeared cloches nothing grew but spindly vegetation. The cuttings did not take; the grafts came unstuck, the sap stopped running in the layers, the trees got white rot in their roots; the seedlings were a desolation. The wind enjoyed blowing down the beanpoles, the strawberries were spoilt from too much manure, the tomatoes from not enough pinching.

He failed with broccoli, aubergines, turnips, and watercress, which he had tried to grow in a tub. After the thaw all the artichokes were lost. The cabbages consoled him. One in particular aroused his hopes. It spread outwards and upwards, finished by being prodigious and absolutely inedible. No matter. Pécuchet was happy to possess such a monster.

> GUSTAVE FLAUBERT
> *BOUVARD AND PÉCUCHET* (1881)

It must at least be confessed that to embellish the form of nature is an innocent amusement.

> SAMUEL JOHNSON
> ON WILLIAM SHENSTONE
> *THE LIVES OF THE POETS* (1781)

8

Seasons

Weekend gardeners may be more aware of the passage of seasons than many of their fellows. As a weekend gardener myself, I have often been struck by the way enormous changes can occur during those few days while we are back in the city. On a Sunday night or Monday morning, as we're leaving the country, it's all winter; by Friday evening—spring has arrived! The same thing happens in autumn: between one weekend and the next every leaf in the place seems to fall. I'm not at all sure that such events would happen so abruptly if we were there to watch.

Still, no one can call himself a gardener who isn't keenly—sometimes monomaniacally—interested in the weather and the seasons of the year. How could springtime be satisfactorily described or celebrated except in terms of growing things? Consciousness of the first frost is a part of every gardener's mindset (also of the fox-hunter—witness Jorrocks' delight upon discovering blackened dahlias, a sure sign that frost had made the ground hard enough for hunting). And nobody but a hydraulic engineer is likely to care as much as a gardener about whether or not it rains when it should. In this regard, by the way, a gardener's (to him reasonable) demands reach a peak of complexity that only Karel Čapek, in his gardener's prayer, has ever spelled out adequately.

Garden writers are fond of claiming that every season is as full of beauties and pleasures as any other. This is of course nonsense. Watching an equinoctial gale toppling the *Verbena bonariensis* and sweeping away the asters, the second flush of penstemon blossoms, the cosmos that came on so late, and all the other autumn flowers; opening the curtains on a March morning to see the magnolia flattened under ten inches of fresh wet snow; peering out from the porch into the sixth dismal day of non-stop May rain—the heart does not merely sink, but bumps along the bottom. Nevertheless, as Henry Mitchell observes, "A gardener must not feel sorry for himself." After all, like everybody else, we always have summer to look forward to.

It would be worthwhile having a cultivated garden if only to see what Autumn does to it.

ALFRED AUSTIN
THE GARDEN THAT I LOVE (1894)

A garden is never so good as it will be next year.

THOMAS COOPER
HORTICULTURE MAGAZINE (JANUARY 1993)

May 31 [1792]. Grass grows very fast. Honey-suckles very fragrant, and most beautiful objects. Columbines make a figure. My white thorn, which hangs over the earth-house, is now one sheet of bloom, and has pendulous boughs down to the ground.

GILBERT WHITE
THE JOURNALS OF GILBERT WHITE (1931)
EDITED BY W. JOHNSON

A gardener must not feel sorry for himself, even in winter, and no matter how great the cause.

HENRY MITCHELL
THE ESSENTIAL EARTHMAN (1981)

"Now is the time to thin out the carrots . . ." [is] an observation which always makes me come out in a cold sweat, when I read it in a London paper. As though the earth were hardening, minute by minute, so that one must rush up to the country and do things before it is too late.

> BEVERLEY NICHOLS
> *DOWN THE GARDEN PATH* (1932)

September . . . what a turnover, what a watershed of the year.

> V. SACKVILLE-WEST
> *MORE FOR YOUR GARDEN* (1955)

We may see on a spring day in one place more beauty in a wood than in any garden.

> WILLIAM ROBINSON
> *THE GARDEN BEAUTIFUL* (1907)

Possibly there is something in the universe which does not work on Sundays and holidays and in this way the eternal order of nature is upset. It might be scientifically ascertained whether trees and grass grow on Sundays and holidays; at the same time it is an empirical fact that on the red-letter days of the calendar it rains more than other days, spiritual activity is at a low ebb, dogs smell worse than usual, and children are a nuisance; then it is windy, lots of people get drowned, and there is an excessive number of motor accidents, actors give a worse performance, trains and trams have a bad service, digestions get upset and beer and literature are worse than at any other time. It is, therefore, possible that Sundays and holidays are based on some peculiar and periodical cosmic disturbance, and that on Sunday mornings I simply wake up with a physical foreboding that something is not as it should be.

KAREL ČAPEK
INTIMATE THINGS (1935)
TRANSLATED BY DORA ROUND

They have climate in England; we have weather.

HELENA RUTHERFURD ELY
A WOMAN'S HARDY GARDEN (1903)

Joy spreads the heart, and with a general song,
Spring issues out, and leads the jolly months along.

JOHN DRYDEN
"THE FLOWER AND THE LEAF"
FABLES ANCIENT AND MODERN (1700)

The blossoms of the apricot
    blow from the east to the west
And I have tried to keep them from falling.

EZRA POUND
THE CANTOS (1970)

No two gardens are the same. No two days are the same in one garden.

HUGH JOHNSON (1939–   )

Autumn arrives in the early morning, but spring at the close of a winter day.

ELIZABETH BOWEN (1899–1973)

The lost leaves measure our years; they are gone as the days are gone.

RICHARD JEFFERIES
THE LIFE OF THE FIELDS (1908)

If it were of any use, every day the gardener would fall on his knees and pray somehow like this: "O Lord, grant that in some way it may rain every day, say from about midnight until three o'clock in the morning, but, you see, it must be gentle and warm so that it can soak in; grant that at the same time it would not rain on campion, alyssum, helianthemum, lavender, and the others which you in your infinite wisdom know are drought-loving plants—I will write their names on a bit of paper if you like— and grant that the sun may shine the whole day long, but not everywhere (not, for instance, on spiraea, or on gentian, plantain lily, and rhododendron), and not too much; that there may be plenty of dew and little wind, enough worms, no plant-lice and snails, no mildew, and that once a week thin liquid manure and guano may fall from heaven. Amen."

KAREL ČAPEK
THE GARDENER'S YEAR
TRANSLATED BY M. AND R. WEATHERALL (1931)

Now that all the other many-hued flowers have scattered without a trace, the dead white head of the miscanthus remains alone in the fields until the end of winter. As it stands there so gracefully, not realizing that it has entered its dotage, and bending its head as if in memory of past glories, it looks exactly like a very old person, and one cannot help feeling sorry for it.

SEI SHŌNAGON
THE PILLOW BOOK OF SEI SHŌNAGON (TENTH CENTURY)
TRANSLATED BY IVAN MORRIS (1967)

Against the uniform sheet of snow and the greyish winter sky the Italian villa loomed up rather grimly; even in summer it kept its distance, and the boldest coleus bed had never ventured nearer than thirty feet from its awful front.

EDITH WHARTON
THE AGE OF INNOCENCE (1920)

Ceanothus blossoms
    and the radiator boiling
        smells of spring.

GARY SNYDER
"I: VI: 40077"
AXE HANDLES (1981)

Freddie Oaker, of the Drones, who does tales of true love for the weeklies under the pen-name of Alicia Seymour, once told me that he reckoned that flowery meadows in springtime were worth at least a hundred quid a year to him.

P. G. WODEHOUSE
THANK YOU JEEVES (1934)

Who can endure a cabbage bed in October?

JANE AUSTEN
SANDITON (WRITTEN 1817)

Hurrah! . . . it is a frost!—the dahlias are dead.

R. S. SURTEES
HANDLEY CROSS (1843)

With daffodils mad footnotes for the spring,
And asters purple asterisks for autumn—

CONRAD AIKEN
PRELUDES FOR MEMNON (1930)

There is really no such thing as bad weather, only different kinds of good weather.

JOHN LUBBOCK, LORD AVEBURY (1834–1913)

9

Enthusiasm

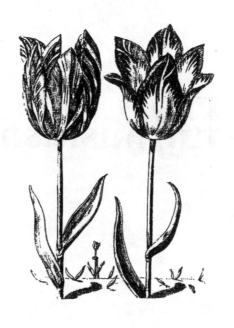

Most of us came on gardening late. Germaine Greer has argued, I don't know how seriously, that this is a matter of hormones; I suspect that economics, rather than dying passions, may have more to do with it. Older people have the money and the time. The fact remains that the best gardeners are hardly young, and that (especially in England) there are plenty of people calmly tending their phlox at an age when the average non-gardener would have long since packed it in. I'm tempted to conclude that there is something literally life-enhancing about the activity.

One reason for this may be what I can only call the spiritual force that gardens and gardening seem capable of evoking in susceptible souls. This shows up most clearly in such writings as Andrew Marvell's dizzying poem *The Garden,* where something very nearly approaching ecstacy is achieved, or the passage about flowers in Christopher Smart's madhouse epic *Jubilate Agno.* The same note, quieter perhaps but no less authentic, sounds in Emerson's description of his "exhilaration" in digging his garden, and Nathaniel Hawthorne's account of simply contemplating his.

While we may not all reach such a pitch of enthusiasm, no gardener is wholly without such feelings of involvement with his or her creation. All the elements—surprise, anticipation, the probability of tangible achievement—encourage this. They are perfectly capable of outweighing disappointments or small disasters. They keep us going back to undertake the next job, to look forward to the next flowering, to enjoy what the garden has in store for us. It may be that to appreciate these joys—to allow the enthusiasm to find expression most purely—we need a certain amount of age on our heads, or at least fewer distractions than youth generally provides.

I am not a greedy person except about flowers and plants, and then I become fanatically greedy.

MAY SARTON (1912–1996)

Like clouds moving across the sky dissolving and re-forming now in towering rounded masses, now in long streamers of curling wraiths, now jagged and torn or neatly spread in fish scale pattern over the sky, my garden's patterns shape and re-shape themselves. A leaf or a twig, the feel of a stone step under one's tread, a trickle of water, the musky smell of a cyclamen plant set in a pot that you have but to tap to know from the sound whether it needs watering or not, such transient impressions as these can open a door and set in motion a whole world of garden pictures. Each second is new and in each second are implicit a hundred gardens. In one it is sunset and suddenly there is a chattering in the pine trees and in the moment of evening's hush eight magpies wing through the air, drop down for a moment among the short grasses where the harebells flower and then, calling to each other, disperse and whirl severally back into the trees. Elsewhere the butterflies, peacocks and red admirals, settle thickly on the purple honey-scented panicles of buddleia. Below the great stone house is a lawn squarely hedged with dark green yew, where a white peacock spreads the splendour of his tail and sets his wing quills drumming. Where a russet brick bridge spans the moat, an old Persian lilac makes a mound of blossom to hang over the moss-green water where later the dragonflies will seem to tease the golden carp.

So, as in a kaleidoscope, the brightly coloured trifles shift and at each turn comes a new garden picture, dimensioned in time as well as space . . .

RUSSELL PAGE
THE EDUCATION OF A GARDENER (1962)

And this is certain; if so be
You could just now my garden see,
The aspic of my flowers so bright
Would make you shudder with delight.

EDWARD LEAR (1812–1888)

Oh, the incredible profit by digging of ground!

THOMAS FULLER
HISTORY OF THE WORTHIES OF ENGLAND (1662)

When I return from trampling on flowers, the hoofs of my horse are fragrant.

> LINE OF A CHINESE POEM
> QUOTED BY CHIANG YEE
> *THE CHINESE EYE* (1935)

That we find a crystal or a poppy beautiful means that we are less alone, that we are more deeply inserted into existence than the course of a single life would lead us to believe.

> JOHN BERGER
> *THE SENSE OF SIGHT* (1980)

I must own that I would do almost anything, and grow almost anything, for the sake of a fragrance.

> REGINALD FARRER
> *IN A YORKSHIRE GARDEN* (1909)

I never had any other desire so strong, and so like to covetousness, as that one which I have had always, that I might be master at last of a small house and a large Garden.

> ABRAHAM COWLEY
> *THE GARDEN* (1666)

He leaped the fence, and saw that all nature was a garden.

HORACE WALPOLE
ON THE LANDSCAPE DESIGNER WILLIAM KENT
ON MODERN GARDENING (1780)

I have caught hold of the earth, to use a gardener's phrase, and neither my friends nor my enemies will find it an easy matter to transplant me again.

HENRY ST. JOHN, LORD BOLINGBROKE (1678–1751)
LETTER TO JONATHAN SWIFT

What wondrous Life in this I lead!
Ripe Apples drop about my head;
The Luscious Clusters of the Vine
Upon my Mouth do crush their Wine;
The Nectaren and curious Peach
Into my hands themselves do reach;
Stumbling on Melons, as I pass,
Insnared with Flowers, I fall on Grass.

Mean while the Mind, from pleasure less,
Withdraws into its happiness:
The Mind, that Ocean, where each kind
Does streight its own resemblance find;
Yet it creates, transcending these,
Far other Worlds, and other Seas,
Annihilating all that's made
To a green Thought in a green Shade.

ANDREW MARVELL
"THE GARDEN"
MISCELLANEOUS POEMS (1681)

My garden, that skirted the avenue of the Manse, was of precisely the right extent. An hour or two of morning labor was all that it required. But I used to visit and revisit it a dozen times a day, and stand in deep contemplation over my vegetable progeny with a love that nobody could share or conceive of, who had never taken part in the process of creation.

NATHANIEL HAWTHORNE
MOSSES FROM AN OLD MANSE (1846)

There is nothing in the world more peaceful than apple-leaves
with an early moon.

ALICE MEYNELL (1847–1922)

Now hath *Flora* rob'd her bowers
To befrend this place with flowers;
    Strowe aboute, strowe aboute,
The Skye rayn'd never kindlyer Showers.

THOMAS CAMPION
MASKE . . . IN HONOUR OF LORD HAYES, AND HIS BRIDE (1607)

The Florentine legend was that he [the poet Walter Savage
Landor] had one day, after an imperfect dinner, thrown the
cook out of the window, and, while the man was writhing with
a broken limb, ejaculated "Good God! I forgot the violets."

RICHARD MONCKTON MILNES, LORD HOUGHTON
MONOGRAPHS (1873)

How magnificent it sounds! That is the fun of writing of one's garden: a steep bank can be a cliff, a puddle a pool, a pool a lake, bog and moraine sound as though a guide were needed to find your way across them, and yet may be covered by a sheet of the *Times*. My Dolomites lie within the compass of my outstretched arms.

EDWARD AUGUSTUS BOWLES
MY GARDEN IN SPRING (1914)

Today I think
Only with scents,—scents dead leaves yield,
And bracken, and wild carrot's seed,
And the square mustard field;

Odours that rise
When the spade wounds the root of a tree,
Rose, currant, raspberry, or goutweed,
Rhubarb or celery;

The smoke's smell, too,
Flowing from where a bonfire burns
The dead, the waste, the dangerous,
And all to sweetness turns . . .

EDWARD THOMAS
"DIGGING"
COLLECTED POEMS (1978)

Walking in the garden
after the benediction of the rain,
my poor, big devil of a nose inhales April.

EDMOND ROSTAND
CYRANO DE BERGERAC (1897)

When I go into my garden with a spade, and dig a bed, I feel
such an exhilaration and health that I discover that I have been
defrauding myself all this time in letting others do for me what
I should have done with my own hands.

RALPH WALDO EMERSON
MAN THE REFORMER (1849)

The collector's dream is to have some illustrious plant to bear
his name immortal through the gardens of future generations,
long after he shall have become dust of their paths. Mere beauty
will not do; for the plant may fail and fade in cultivation, and
his name be no more known, except to the learned, as attached
to a dead dry sliver on the sheets of a herbarium. To become
vividly immortal in the Valhalla of gardeners, one must own a

species as vigorous as it is glorious, a thing capable of becoming and remaining a household word among English enthusiasts.

REGINALD FARRER
THE RAINBOW BRIDGE (1921)

Many of the ancients do poorly live in the single names of Vegetables.

SIR THOMAS BROWNE
THE GARDEN OF CYRUS (1658)

For there is no Height in which there are not flowers.
For flowers have great virtues for all the senses.
For the flower glorifies God and the root parries the
   adversary.
For the flowers have their angels even the words of God's
   Creation.
For the warp and woof of flowers are worked by perpetual
   moving spirits.
For flowers are good both for the living and the dead.
For there is a language of flowers.

For there is sound reasoning upon all flowers.
For elegant phrases are nothing but flowers.
For flowers are peculiarly the poetry of Christ.
For flowers are medicinal.
For flowers are musical in ocular harmony.
For the right names of flowers are yet in heaven.
    God made gardners better nomenclators.
    For the Poorman's nosegay is an introduction to a
    Prince.

CHRISTOPHER SMART
JUBILATE AGNO (1758–1763, PUBLISHED 1939)

Our pleasant labour to reform
Yon flourie arbor, yonder allies green,
Our walks at noon with branches overgrown.

JOHN MILTON
PARADISE LOST (1667)

I think the true gardener is a lover of his flowers, not a critic of them. I think the true gardener is the reverent servant of Nature, not her truculent, wife-beating master. I think the true gardener, the older he grows, should more and more develop a humble, grateful and uncertain spirit.

REGINALD FARRER
IN A YORKSHIRE GARDEN (1909)

The garden, like beauty in landscape, is inimical to all evil passions: it stands for efficiency, for patience in labour, for strength in adversity, for the power to forgive.

SIR GEORGE SITWELL
ON THE MAKING OF GARDENS (1909)

The pride of my heart and the delight of my eyes is my garden. Our house, which is in dimensions very much like a bird-cage, and might, with almost equal convenience, be laid on a shelf, or hung up in a tree, would be utterly unbearable in warm weather, were it not that we have a retreat out of doors.

MARY RUSSELL MITFORD
OUR VILLAGE (1832)

10

Edible and Inedible

The subject here is vegetables and weeds. (Technically, I suppose, it isn't fair to call weeds inedible; you can eat some of them—nettles, for instance—though I wouldn't go out of my way to do so.) We gardeners spend a lot of time encouraging the one and trying to get rid of the other, so it seemed to make sense to lump quotes on the two of them together.

I've always felt more comfortable gardening with vegetables than with flowers. Possibly this is because I am at heart a hunter-gatherer (I also like to fish, and to eat what I catch) and my approach to horticulture is via the kitchen. My first garden, in Michigan in 1943, was a vegetable garden. Nominally a "Victory Garden," it was in fact a thoroughgoing defeat. I dug it behind the garage. The earth dried into large brick-like clumps that I tried and failed to smash into workable tilth. Many years later, assisted by a large roto-tiller from my brother-in-law, whose company made them, I had better luck with vegetables in the Berkshires, where I fed a large population of woodchucks and deer. These days, in Britain, I grow a respectable crop of asparagus, unusual potatoes, beans, perpetual spinach, and a few other useful odds and ends like lettuce, rocket, green onions, and parsley.

One thing that's nice about vegetable gardening is that design doesn't come into it. I'm aware that there is a movement in favor of ornamental vegetable beds—*potagers* and all that—but I'm not tempted to get involved. There is something seriously perverse about forcing such an earnest and innocent plant as a stalk of sweet corn to take center stage in a composition suited to the eye of a Renaissance Frenchman. And the box hedging! If life is too short to peel a grape, it is certainly too short to grow cabbages in the form of a quincunx.

Because I don't have to worry about design in my vegetable garden, I can go right down the rows chopping weeds with a hoe and raking them up. It may not be beautiful, but it's efficient. And since vegetables do not do a very good job of shading out weeds, there are plenty of them, some quite exotic. An inadequately heated compost pile, which fails to kill off weed seeds, plus the use of sheep manure (it comes free, but is also full of seeds) explains why.

As for weeding elsewhere in the garden, I share with Gertrude Jekyll a sense of the pleasure to be gained from this methodical pastime, especially when the ground is moist and loose, and even a buttercup comes up with all its long white roots intact. Dock, of course, with a taproot that is reaching for the Mohorovičić Discontinuity, is another matter.

One cannot have enough
Of this delicious stuff.

E. V. Rieu
"Soliloquy of a Tortoise on Revisiting the Lettuce Beds
After an Interval of One Hour While Supposed to be
Sleeping in a Clump of Blue Hollyhocks"
A Puffin Quartet of Poets (1958)

Garden raddishes are in wantoness by the gentry eaten as a sallad,
but they breed but scurvy humours in the stomach, and corrupt
the blood, and then send for a physician as fast as you can.

Nicholas Culpeper
The Compleat Herbal (1653)

As a mere vegetable or sauce, as the country people call it, [the
potato] does very well to qualify the effect of fat meat, or to
assist in the swallowing of quantities of butter.

William Cobbett
The English Gardener (1838)

In Garden Delights t'is not easy to hold a Mediocritie; that insinuating pleasure is seldome without some extremity. The Antients venially delighted in flourishing Gardens; many were Florists that knew not the true use of a Flower . . . Some commendably affected Plantations of venemous Vegetables, some confined their delights unto single plants, and Cato seemed to dote upon Cabbadge; While the ingenious delights of Tulipists stands saluted with hard language, even by their own Professors.

SIR THOMAS BROWNE
"EPISTLE DEDICATORY" TO *THE GARDEN OF CYRUS* (1658)

To get the best results you must talk to your vegetables.

PRINCE CHARLES
QUOTED IN *THE OBSERVER* (SEPTEMBER 1986)

It seems to me an utter waste of words to argue whether vegetables, if of one genus or an identical kind, are species or varieties.

WILLIAM HERBERT
AMARYLLIDACEAE, WITH A TREATISE ON CROSS-BRED VEGETABLES (1837)

This is the result of my experience in raising beans: Plant the common small white bush bean about the first of June, in rows three feet by eighteen inches apart, being careful to select fresh round and unmixed seed. First look out for worms, and supply vacancies by planting anew. Then look out for woodchucks, if it is an exposed place, for they will nibble off the earliest tender leaves almost clean as they go; and again, when the young tendrils make their appearance, they have notice of it, and will shear them off with both buds and young pods, sitting erect like a squirrel. But above all harvest as early as possible, if you would escape frosts and have a fair and saleable crop; you may save much loss by this means.

HENRY DAVID THOREAU
WALDEN (1854)

How cucumbers along the surface creep,
With crooked bodies, and with bellies deep.

VIRGIL
GEORGICS
TRANSLATED BY JOHN DRYDEN (1697)

Cabbage. A familiar garden vegetable about as large and wise as a man's head.

AMBROSE BIERCE
THE ENLARGED DEVIL'S DICTIONARY (1906)

A cauliflower is a cabbage with a college education.

MARK TWAIN (1835–1910)

I want death to find me planting my cabbages.

MICHEL DE MONTAIGNE (1533–1592)

If you plant a good turnip seed properly a turnip is what you will get every single time.

RUTH STOUT
HOW TO HAVE A GREEN THUMB WITHOUT AN ACHING BACK (1955)

What I claim is the fastest asparagus. As for eating purposes,
I have seen better.

CHARLES DUDLEY WARNER
MY SUMMER IN A GARDEN (1871)

Tomatoes and squash never fail to reach maturity. You can spray
them with acid, beat them with sticks and burn them; they love
it.

S. J. PERELMAN
ACRES AND PAINS (1951)

What would the world be, once bereft
Of wet and wildness? Let them be left,
O let them be left, wildness and wet;
Long live the weeds and the wilderness yet.

GERARD MANLEY HOPKINS
"INVERSNAID" (1881)
POEMS (1918)

There is some hope in weeding, for the weeds may one day be defeated, but the tidying of a garden is as exacting and unending as the daily washing of dishes.

> CLARE LEIGHTON
> FOUR HEDGES (1935)

Nothing is so interesting as weeding. I went crazy over the outdoor work, and had at last to confine myself to the house, or literature must have gone by the board.

> ROBERT LOUIS STEVENSON
> LETTER TO SIR SIDNEY COLVIN FROM SAMOA, 1890
> QUOTED IN *ROBERT LOUIS STEVENSON* (1993)
> FRANK McLYNN

There, fed by Food they love, to rankest size,
Around the Dwellings *Dock* and *Wormwood* rise;
Here the strong *Mallow* strikes her slimy Root,
Here the dull *Nightshade* hangs her deadly fruit;
On hills of Dust the *Henbane*'s faded green,
And pencil'd Flower of sickly scent is seen;

At the Wall's base the fiery Nettle springs,
With Fruit globose and fierce with poison'd Stings;
Above (the Growth of many a Year) is spread
The yellow Level of the *Stone-crop*'s Bed;
In every Chink delights the *Fern* to grow,
With glossy Leaf and tawny Bloom below:
These, with our *Sea-weeds*, rolling up and down,
Form the contracted *Flora* of the Town.

GEORGE CRABBE
THE BOROUGH (1810)

In the garden, the usual foreigners gave place to the most scarce
flowers, and especially to the rarer weed, of Britain; and these
were scattered here and there only for preservation . . . My
father . . . passed much of his time among his choice weeds.

GEORGE CRABBE [THE YOUNGER]
LIFE OF THE REV. GEORGE CRABBE (1844)

The gardener has a great faith in names; a flower without a name, to put it platonically, is a flower without a metaphysical idea; in short, it has not a right and absolute reality. A flower without a name is a weed.

KAREL ČAPEK
THE GARDENER'S YEAR
TRANSLATED BY M. AND R. WEATHERALL (1931)

My garden claims a good part of my spare time in the middle of the day, when I am not engaged at home or taking a walk; there is always something to interest me even in the very sight of the weeds and the litter, for then I think how much improved the place will be when they are removed.

THOMAS ARNOLD
LETTER TO J. T. COLERIDGE, 1819

Flowers in my time which everyone would praise,
Though thrown like weeds from gardens nowadays.

JOHN CLARE (1793–1864)

I always think of my sins when I weed. They grow apace in the same way and are harder still to get rid of.

HELENA RUTHERFURD ELY
A WOMAN'S HARDY GARDEN (1903)

The frost hurts not weeds.

THOMAS FULLER
GNOMOLOGIA (1732)

One is tempted to say that the most human plants, after all, are the weeds.

JOHN BURROUGHS
PEPACTON (1881)

A good garden may have some weeds.

ANONYMOUS

Many gardeners will agree that hand-weeding is not the terrible drudgery that it is often made out to be. Some people find in it a kind of soothing monotony. It leaves their minds free to develop the plot for their next novel or to perfect the brilliant repartee with which they should have encountered a relative's latest example of unreasonableness.

CHRISTOPHER LLOYD
THE WELL-TEMPERED GARDEN (1973)

Weeding is a delightful occupation, especially after summer rain, when the roots come up clear and clean. One gets to know how many and various are the ways of weeds—as many almost as the moods of human creatures.

GERTRUDE JEKYLL
WOOD AND GARDEN (1899)

Perhaps if we could penetrate Nature's secrets we should find that what we call weeds are more essential to the well-being of the world, than the most precious fruit or grain.

NATHANIEL HAWTHORNE
OUR OLD HOME (1863)

A gardener who knows his flowers and is ignorant of weeds now seems to me to be like half a coin, a tail without a head.

SARA STEIN
MY WEEDS (1988)

The gardener's cat is dead, the gardener gone
And last year's garden grows salacious weeds.

WALLACE STEVENS
"CREDENCES OF SUMMER"
TRANSPORT TO SUMMER (1947)

A weed is a plant that is not only in the wrong place, but intends to stay.

SARA STEIN
MY WEEDS (1988)

A garden is an awful responsibility. You never know what you may be aiding to grow in it.

CHARLES DUDLEY WARNER
MY SUMMER IN A GARDEN (1871)

All the pessimism of a Schopenhauer
    is implicit in the garden-lover's creed:
that whatever needs attention is a flower,
    and whatever grows without it is a weed.

PIET HEIN
"GOD WOT"
GROOKS VI (1978)

Not all seedlings are weeds. You may feel that life is too short
to leave a seedling in till it's large enough to identify. My own
feeling is that life's too interesting not to leave it there until you
can identify it.

CHRISTOPHER LLOYD
THE WELL-TEMPERED GARDEN (1973)

Where does weed wisdom reside? Plants have no brains. They
have no nerves. They don't have ears or eyes. Their intelligence
resides in community and consensus, in each cell's relating to
its neighbors what limited information it has, and, within a
mesh of influencing neighbors, making its individual decisions.

SARA STEIN
MY WEEDS (1988)

II

Consolations

Failures happen. Black spot attacks the roses, mildew the lilac, the white penstemon turns out to be a sickly pink. Droughts, floods, wireworm in the potatoes, rabbits in the bush beans, a herd of cows making a quagmire of the lawn. It simply isn't fair. And then there are the errors of judgment you can blame on no one but yourself—the string trimmer that girdles the baby tree peony or lops the clematis, the over-fertilized *Sedum spectabile* that flops on the *Salvia ulignosa,* the retaining wall built on inadequate footing. Who has avoided such calamities? (Not I— I've had them all.)

Fortunately, a kindly God of gardeners offers us consolation for our misfortune. Disasters are rarely permanent (although in Henry Mitchell's view "disaster . . . is the normal state for any garden.") The wall can be rebuilt, the roses can be sprayed, the clematis will come back another year (or can be replanted). The important thing is not to take it personally. It most likely isn't your fault anyway. As Eleanor Perényi observes, "A garden isn't a testing ground for character."

It may take a while to attain this sort of philosophical detachment. Some of us never will. We will go right on thinking that if we had only watered the dahlias more (or less) they would have bloomed properly, or blaming ourselves for the virus in the raspberries. Yet perfection is not only unattainable, especially in a garden, but according to the Japanese it is actually blasphemous. Our failures only prove that we are human. In a way, I suppose, that is a test of character too, but a healthier one. Brooding over what we have done wrong, what nature has done wrong, or what some recalcitrant little flower has done wrong, is more than a waste of time, it is a contradiction in principle. Plants, as Anne Raver reminds us, don't carry grudges, so why should we?

An established plant becomes a heirloom, for in all likelihood it will outlive the gardener who plants it.

ELIZABETH LAWRENCE
A SOUTHERN GARDEN (1942)

I detect an unwholesome strain in gardeners here, who keep forgetting how very favorable our climate is, and who seem almost on the verge of ingratitude. Disaster, they must learn, is the normal state for any garden.

HENRY MITCHELL
THE ESSENTIAL EARTHMAN (1981)

It takes a while to grasp that not all failures are self-imposed, the result of ignorance, carelessness or inexperience. It takes a while to grasp that a garden isn't a testing ground for character and to stop asking, what did I do wrong? Maybe nothing.

ELEANOR PERÉNYI
GREEN THOUGHTS (1981)

"Why, Sir, they have as good a right to live as we; they are our fellow worms."

HENRY WADSWORTH LONGFELLOW'S LANDLADY
WHEN CANKERWORMS DROPPED ON HER TURBAN, CA. 1840
QUOTED IN *AMERICAN GARDENS OF THE NINETEENTH CENTURY* (1987)
ANNE LEIGHTON

A Gardener's life
Is full of sweets and sours;
He gets the sunshine
When he needs the showers.

REGINALD ARKELL
"COMPENSATION"
GREEN FINGERS (1935)

Nothing in the garden is really difficult. Everything can be managed by an ordinary imbecile; indeed, that is why it is the greatest of all amusements.

HENRY MITCHELL
HENRY MITCHELL ON GARDENING (1998)

I value my garden more for being full of blackbirds than cherries, and very frankly give them fruit for their song.

JOSEPH ADDISON
THE SPECTATOR (1712)

As to the garden, it seems to me its chief fruit is—blackbirds.

WILLIAM MORRIS
LETTER TO HIS DAUGHTER JENNY, AUGUST 24, 1888
THE COLLECTED LETTERS OF WILLIAM MORRIS (1987)
EDITED BY NORMAN KELVIN

Gardening, above all crafts, is a matter of faith, grounded, however (if on nothing better), on his experience that somehow or other seasons go on in their right course, and bring their right results.

CANON HENRY ELLACOMBE
IN A GLOUCESTERSHIRE GARDEN (1897)

Plants don't point a finger. If they live, they don't carry grudges. If they die, unless you've killed an entire species or a rain forest, you feel only momentary guilt, which is quickly replaced by a philosophical, smug feeling: Failure is enriching your compost pile.

ANNE RAVER
DEEP IN THE GREEN (1995)

A killing frost devastates the heart as well as the garden.

ELEANOR PERÉNYI
GREEN THOUGHTS (1981)

Your spring is passed in anxious doubts and fears, which are usually realized; and so a great moral discipline is worked out for you.

CHARLES DUDLEY WARNER
MY SUMMER IN A GARDEN (1871)

When you have done your best for a flower, and it fails, you have some reason to be aggrieved.

FRANK SWINNERTON
TOKEFIELD PAPERS (1949)

Gardening has compensations out of all proportion to its goals. It is creation in the pure sense.

PHYLLIS MCGINLEY
THE PROVINCE OF THE HEART (1959)

One thing that unites all gardeners as they contemplate the compost heap is a belief in reincarnation, at least for plants.

GEOFFREY CHARLESWORTH
THE OPINIONATED GARDENER (1988)

I used to be ashamed of how much waste there was even in my unpretentious garden here. I blamed inexperience, impatience and extravagance. But now I have come to accept that one must not count the losses, they would be too alarming. One must count only the joys, and feel continually blessed in them. There is no unlucky gardener, for each small success outweighs each defeat in his or her passionate heart.

MAY SARTON
PLANT DREAMING DEEP (1968)

A Who's Who
of Those Quoted

Ackerman, Diane: American poet and essayist.

Adams, John (1735–1826): Second president of the United States, founder of a dynasty.

Addison, Joseph (1672–1719): Essayist, praised by Dr. Johnson as "the model of the middle style," apparently a rather hectic gardener.

Aiken, Conrad (1889–1973): American poet, college classmate of T. S. Eliot at Harvard, but a less good and certainly less successful writer.

Albert, Prince (1819–1861): Queen Victoria's husband.

Alberti, Leon Battista degli (1404–1472): Renaissance architect and theorist.

Alcott, Amos Bronson (1799–1888): One of the many sages of nineteenth-century Concord, Massachusetts. Father of Louisa May Alcott.

Allen, Woody (1935–   ): A noted non-gardener.

Anglicus, Bartholomaeus: Thirteenth-century scientist-monk.

Anonymous: Author of many often contradictory apothegms.

Arkell, Reginald: English poet specializing in amiable light verse about gardens.

Arnold, Thomas (1795–1842): Father of Matthew Arnold, a great educational reformer as headmaster of Rugby School, author of several works of Roman history.

Aubrey, John (1626–1697): Cranky memorialist, whose biographical sketches of many of the leading figures of his time make irresistible reading for their pungency and humor.

Auden, W. H. (1907–1973): English poet, long resident in New York, author of numerous volumes of elegant and fascinating verse along with criticism, opera librettos, and other works.

Austen, Jane (1775–1817): The best novelist in English before George Eliot (and possibly afterward).

Austin, Alfred (1835–1913): Dim poet, author of a pleasant prose work about his garden that became a best-seller, after which he was appointed to succeed Tennyson as Poet Laureate (to great mockery and derision).

Bacon, Francis (1561–1626): Lawyer, politician, philosopher, and universal genius of the Elizabethan era. His scientific bent led to his demise, of a cold contracted while stuffing a chicken with snow.

Bakalar, Elsa: American author of a book about flower gardening.

Barrie, J. M. (1860–1937): Terminally twee author of such successes as *Peter Pan*.

Bates, Herbert Ernest (1905–1974): Prolific and highly successful English novelist and short-story writer.

Beckford, William (1759–1844): Eccentric, colossally rich dilettante who managed finally to bankrupt himself building gardens, houses, and towers (one of which collapsed almost as soon as it was completed). But he also wrote—a gothic romance called *Vathek*, and some wonderful accounts of travels in Portugal, Spain, and Italy.

Beecher, Henry (1813–1887): Charismatic American preacher and lecturer who came a cropper over a woman and ended up in court charged with adultery.

Belloc, Hilaire (1870–1953): Powerfully opinionated British journalist, author of many books and much verse, most of it light and/or satirical.

Berger, John (1926–   ): Novelist and art critic.

Bierce, Ambrose (1842–1914?): Sardonic American writer responsible for many fine short stories and journalism; went off to Mexico at the end of his life and disappeared.

Blake, William (1757–1827): God-possessed English poet and artist.

Boswell, James (1740–1795): The great biographer of Dr. Johnson and magnificent, if inadvertent, autobiographer.

Bowen, Elizabeth (1899–1973): Anglo-Irish novelist, especially skillful at describing places and landscapes; *Bowen's Court*, the book she wrote about her family's ancestral mansion in County Cork, is a delicious blend of history and reminiscence.

Bowles, Edward Augustus (1865–1954): One of this century's most charming and knowledgeable garden writers, creator of a splendid garden at Myddleton House near London, which survives, and three books about it.

Boyle, E. V. (1825–1916): Woman writer of romantic books about gardens and gardening under several pseudonyms.

Brackenbury, Robin: English writer.

Brautigan, Richard (1935–1984): Off-beat American short-story writer and novelist, popular in the 1960s.

Browne, Sir Thomas (1605–1682): A doctor turned writer, who apart from religious works, mostly gloomy, produced a number of unclassifiable literary oddities including *The Garden of Cyrus*. This contains meditations on, among other things, ancient horticultural practices.

Burne-Jones, Edward (1833–1898): English painter and designer, colleague of William Morris.

Burney, Fanny (1752–1840): Novelist, letter-writer and diarist. She married General d'Arblay, a refugee from the French Revolution, and wrote delightfully about their experiences attempting to live a frugal country life.

Burroughs, John (1837–1921): The original American Green.

Byatt, A. S. (1936–   ): Learned English novelist and critic, whose most famous book is probably *Possession*.

Campion, Thomas (1567–1620): Poet, musician, and doctor, author of several lovely books of songs.

Čapek, Karel (1890–1938): Czech essayist and playwright, best known to gardeners as the author of an infinitely quotable little book called *The Gardener's Year.*

Carroll, Lewis (1832–1898): Pen name of C. L. Dodgson, Oxford mathematician, author of *Alice in Wonderland* and other books, and photographer of little girls.

Carson, Rachel (1907–1964): American zoologist and pioneer warrior against pesticides and other threats to the natural world; author of *Silent Spring.*

Cather, Willa (1896–1947): American novelist of the Midwest.

Charles, Prince (1948–   ): The presumed next king of Great Britain, a devoted gardener (organic).

Charlesworth, Geoffrey: Retired American college professor who now lives and gardens in the testing climate of western Massachusetts, in downtimes writing precise and entertaining books dealing largely with alpines.

Chaucer, Geoffrey (1343–1400): Poet, story-teller, and creator, in *The Canterbury Tales,* of a whole unforgettable world.

Chiang Yee: Twentieth-century Chinese artist and writer (in English), author of several attractive travel books illustrated with his own watercolors (*The Silent Traveler in London*, etc.).

Church, Thomas: Garden architect, father of the California style of garden design, who died in 1978.

Clare, John (1793–1864): Born in rural Northamptonshire, a hedge-setter and day-laborer, he achieved brief fame as a peasant poet in 1820 with his *Poems Descriptive of Rural Life and Scenery*, then sank into madness and obscurity. His keenly observed poetry, much of it about nature, was rediscovered only this century.

Cobbett, William (1763–1835): Vigorous writer on all manner of things, including gardening, Cobbett had an inexplicable hatred of potatoes.

Coles, William (1626–1662): Botanist, writer on the medical use of herbs.

Colette (1873–1954): Mononomial French writer (her first names, never used, were Sidonie Gabrielle), author of novels and exquisite memoirs of her childhood in the countryside.

Cooper, Thomas: Author, editor of *Horticulture* magazine.

Cowley, Abraham (1618–1667): English poet.

Cowper, William (1731–1800): Afflicted much of his life by melancholy and hypochondria, Cowper found solace in his garden, and wrote letters and poems that show a deep appreciation of nature.

Crabbe, George (1754–1832): Gloomy, tough-minded chronicler of village life as it really was in early nineteenth-century England. Best known for his tale of *Peter Grimes,* upon which Benjamin Britten based his opera, Crabbe studied botany and had a scientist's eye for plants. Father of **George Crabbe the Younger**.

Crowe, Sylvia (1901–   ): English landscape designer, writer on landscape architecture and ecology. Her *Garden Design* is a standard text.

Culpeper, Nicholas (1616–1664): Botanist, author of an influential early herbal.

Darwin, Charles (1809–1882): Naturalist, writer, thinker, author of *Origin of Species* and the theory of evolution. Darwin had an endearing curiosity about practically everything; he was particularly fond of earthworms.

Davy, Sir Humphry (1778–1829): Chemist, inventor, genius. *The Dictionary of National Biography*, after recounting his extraordinary achievements, says simply: "Died, worn out, Geneva, 1829."

Day, Clarence (1874–1935): Popular American humorist, best known for his book *Life with Father*.

De Ligne, Charles Joseph, Prince (1735–1814): Austrian field marshal famed for his wit and cosmopolitanism. His memoirs run to forty volumes. He created a large and beautiful garden at Beloeil, his Belgian estate, and wrote about it.

Dickens, Charles (1812–1870): Productive and marvelous novelist.

Disraeli, Benjamin (1804–1881): Novelist, politician, prime minister. He famously dismissed George Eliot's *Daniel Deronda* with the remark, "When I want to read a novel I write one."

D'Israeli, Isaac (1766–1848): Father of Benjamin, author of numerous books including particularly *Curiosities of Literature;* a magpie of odd facts.

Douglas, David (1799–1834): Indefatigable plant collector in remote places. His career came to a premature end when he fell into a cattle trap in Hawaii and was gored by the bull that had preceded him.

Downing, Andrew Jackson (1815–1852): Landscape designer and writer on gardens and architecture. Called, rather excessively, "the greatest figure in American horticulture."

Dryden, John (1631–1700): English poet and playwright; Gerard Manley Hopkins called him "the most masculine of all our poets."

Earle, Mrs. C. W. (1836–1925): Author of several volumes of garden lore entitled *Pot Pourri from a Surrey Garden;* sometimes flimsy but often useful and entertaining.

Eddison, Sydney (1932–   ): American gardening writer.

Eden, Emily (1797–1869): Minor novelist, also author of wonderful letters describing her travels in India.

Eliot, George (1819–1880): Pen name of Mary Ann (later Marian) Evans, author of what may be the best novel ever written in the English language, *Middlemarch*.

Ellacombe, Canon Henry (1822–1916): Famous gardening cleric and author of several delightful books about gardening and plants.

Ely, Helena Rutherfurd (1858–1920): One of several skilled American woman gardeners and gardening writers in the early twentieth century.

Emerson, Ralph Waldo (1803–1882): The original Transcendentalist, poet, essayist, and man of great good sense.

Empson, William (1906–1984): English critic (*Seven Types of Ambiguity*) and poet (largely ambiguous).

Evelyn, John (1620–1706): Like his contemporary Samuel Pepys, a great diarist, but also a great gardener and writer on gardens.

Fairchild, Thomas (1667?–1729): London nurseryman and florist. First to discover the existence of sex in plants.

Farrer, Reginald (1880–1920): Plant-hunter, bad novelist, enormously fluent writer on plants, especially alpines.

Fish, Margery: English gardening writer, best known for her book *We Made a Garden*.

Flaubert, Gustave (1821–1880): French novelist, author of *Madame Bovary*. He, his publisher, and his printer were tried for corrupting public morals after its publication, but acquitted, which seems entirely appropriate. *Bouvard and Pécuchet* is an intensely funny satire on contemporary bourgeois life.

Fletcher, H. L. V.: Journeyman twentieth-century English writer on gardening and topography.

Frost, Robert (1874–1963): New England poet, highly popular in America but basically uncongenial.

Fujiwara no Yasusue: Twelfth-century Japanese courtier-poet.

Fuller, Thomas (1608–1661): English clergyman, chaplain to Charles II after the Restoration, writer of lengthy histories.

Garden, Alexander (1730?–1791): American botanist (later settled in England) who introduced many new plants. Gardenia named after him.

Gardener's Chronicle, The: Founded 1841, the most important gardening magazine in Britain during the nineteenth century and after.

Genesis: First book of the Bible.

Gentil, Francis: Seventeenth-century French garden writer.

Gerard, John (1545–1612): Plantsman, herbalist, and plagiarist. He once surreptitiously planted peonies in the wild in England so that he could claim to have found a new native species.

Gilpin, William (1724–1804): Schoolmaster, biographer, and traveler, who toured Great Britain looking for the most authentically picturesque views, and then produced several illustrated books discussing them.

Grigson, Geoffrey (1905–1985): Poet, critic, and editor with a deep knowledge of gardening and plants; in *The Englishman's Flora* he surveyed the whole spectrum of British native species and assembled thousands of local and traditional names for them. A fascinating book.

Hall, John (1529?–1566?): Minor poet and author of medical tracts.

Hamilton, Geoff (1936–1996): For many years Britain's most famous gardener due to his position as presenter of the most important television gardening program. An amiable, down-to-earth fellow, he also produced hundreds of newspaper columns and magazine articles, as well as half a dozen best-selling books.

Harbison, Robert (1940–   ): American writer on architecture and cultural history.

Hawthorne, Nathaniel (1804–1864): Major American novelist and short-story writer. "I have seen so little of the world," he once wrote (in a letter to Longfellow), "that I have nothing but thin air to concoct my stories of." We should all have such air.

Hearn, Lafcadio (1850–1904): American journalist who made his name writing about Japan, where he settled in 1890, marrying a Japanese wife, adopting Japanese dress and a Japanese name (Yakumo Koizumi), but never learning Japanese.

Hedde, Jean Claude Philippe Isidore (1801–1880): French businessman and traveler who was in China from 1843 to 1846 and wrote a book describing what he found there.

Hein, Piet: Modern Danish writer known for his witty short poems called "grooks."

Helps, Sir Arthur (1813–1875): Prolific English author on a variety of subjects. Edited (and probably rewrote) Queen Victoria's books for her.

Herbert, A. P. (1890–1971): Longtime *Punch* contributor and member of Parliament, noted for his light verse.

Herbert, George (1593–1633): Religious poet in Latin and English. His *Outlandish Proverbs* is a collection of foreign proverbs in translation.

Herbert, William (1778–1847): English botanist.

Herrigel, Gustie L.: Like her husband Eugen, author of *Zen and the Art of Archery*, she was born in Germany and became an expert on Japanese Zen Buddhism.

Hogg, Thomas (1792–1862): A friend of Shelley and author of a somewhat undependable life of the poet.

Hollander, John: American poet with a taste for gardens and natural history; he compiled an anthology of garden poetry in 1996.

Home, Henry, Lord Kames (1696–1782): Scottish judge and laird, who wrote on farming, law, religion, and history.

Hopkins, Gerard Manley (1844–1889): Psychologically tormented Catholic priest, whose extraordinary poems were written over the course of many years but went virtually unpublished until long after his death.

Hornby, Sir Simon (1934–   ): British businessman, now president of the Royal Horticultural Society.

Housman, A. E. (1859–1936): Classical scholar, Oxford don, first published the poems in *A Shropshire Lad* at his own expense.

Howitt, William (1792–1879): Forgotten English writer, author of such plausible works as *The Popular History of Priestcraft* and *The Rural and Domestic Life of Germany*.

Hudson, William Henry (1841–1922): English naturalist and writer born and brought up in Argentina.

Hughes, Ted (1930–1998): Brilliant English poet whose work deals particularly with the natural world; Poet Laureate from 1984 until his death, effectively redeeming the seriousness of the position.

Hugo, Victor (1802–1885): French novelist and playwright, author of many books, including *Les Misérables.*

Hunt, Henry Holman (1827–1910): English painter, one of the principal founders of the group known as the Pre-Raphaelite Brotherhood.

Ingalls, John J. (1833–1900): United States Congressman, orator, and essayist.

James, Henry (1843–1916): Who would have thought *he* was a gardener?

Jefferies, Richard (1848–1887): Unsuccessful novelist, engaging and splendidly observant writer on natural history and the English countryside.

Jefferson, Thomas (1743–1826): Third President of the United States and a devoted gardener, both by his own admission

and by the evidence still to be found in the gardens of
Monticello, his handsome estate perched on a mountaintop
near Charlottesville, Virginia.

Jekyll, Gertrude (1843–1932): Long-lived, hugely influential
English gardener, garden designer, and writer about gardening,
responsible (with William Robinson, q.v.) for creating the
dominant garden style of the twentieth century.

Jensen, Jens (1860–1951): Curmudgeonly American landscape
architect, progenitor of the Prairie Style.

Johnson, Hugh (1939–   ): English gardening writer and wine
expert.

Johnson, Louisa: Nineteenth-century American garden writer
who did much to encourage women to take up ornamental
gardening.

Johnson, Samuel (1709–1784): English writer, lexicographer, and
critic with an influence far beyond his writings. A non-pareil
talker, his conversational sallies on all subjects were collected
and treasured, even when the opinions they embodied were
dubious. Johnson was convinced, for example, that swallows
"conglobulate together" at the bottoms of rivers in the winter,
and emerge again each spring.

Joyce, James (1882–1941): Irish novelist, author of *Ulysses.* E. M. Forster called it "a dogged attempt to cover the universe with mud," but he was sadly wrong.

Juvenal (c.60–c.136): Furious Roman satirical poet.

Keane, Molly (1904–1996): Irish novelist with an edge to her tongue.

Keats, John (1795–1821): English lyric poet who died tragically young. Possibly apocryphally, his last words were "I feel the flowers growing over me."

Kellaway, Deborah: English garden writer with several books to her credit and an anthology, *The Virago Book of Women Gardeners.*

Kennedy, Des (1945–   ): Canadian garden writer.

Ki no Tsurayuki: Tenth-century Japanese poet-official, whose poems have been preserved in several famous collections. The *Tosa Diary* describes his return to Kyoto and his ruined garden after years away serving as governor in a remote prefecture.

Kipling, Rudyard (1865–1936): Popular poet and novelist.

Lacy, Allen (1935–   ): American author of a number of gardening books and essays.

Lamb, Charles (1775–1834): Extremely amiable English essayist and minor poet.

Lane Fox, Robin (1946–): English garden writer (gardening correspondent for the *Financial Times*) as well as a brilliant and learned classical scholar and author of several works of history and biography.

Langham, William: Obscure sixteenth-century English medical herbalist.

Lawrence, D. H. (1885–1930): Powerful English novelist, poet, painter, and literary trouble-maker (*Lady Chatterley's Lover* was not the only one of his works to be charged with obscenity).

Lawrence, Elizabeth (1904–1985): Fine American garden writer, author of half a dozen books mainly about gardening in the Middle South. Many of her books have been reprinted, fortunately, by the University of North Carolina Press.

Lawrence, John (died 1732): English writer on gardening; also published sermons.

Lawson, William: Sixteenth-century gardening expert; when he published his charming book on orchard-keeping in 1618, he claimed that it was based on forty-eight years' experience.

Lear, Edward (1812–1888): Jabberwockist.

Le Blond, Alexandre (1679–1719): When John James translated *The Theory and Practice of Gardening* from the French in 1712, he credited the original to Le Blond. In fact the author was the lengthily named Frenchman Antoine-Joseph Dazallier d'Argenville, a garden designer and expert on rocks, while Le Blond was responsible only for some of the plates. The error has persisted ever since, through many reprints and editions.

Lee, Laurie (1914–1998): Author of the classic account of an English country boyhood *Cider with Rosie* and many other works.

Leighton, Clare (1899–1989): Woodcut artist and author, writer on life in rural England and (later) the United States.

Lincoln, Abraham (1809–1865): President, magnificent prose stylist.

Lindbergh, Anne Morrow (1906–   ): Wife of Charles Lindbergh, author of several volumes of memoirs and meditations.

Liu Yin (1249–1293): Confucian scholar and poet.

Lloyd, Christopher (1921–   ): Britain's most respected modern gardening writer, author of numerous books and many articles, proprietor of the magnificent gardens of Great Dixter in East Sussex.

Loudon, Jane Webb (1807–1858): Scarcely less productive than her husband, she did much to encourage women to take up gardening.

Loudon, John Claudius (1783–1843): Unstoppable gardening journalist who produced millions of words on all aspects of the art in books and magazines. Doubtlessly the greatest force in British gardening for nearly fifty years, he eventually wrote himself into the grave.

Lowell, James Russell (1819–1891): American poet, editor, and polemicist.

Lubbock, John, Lord Avebury (1834–1913): Victorian gentleman scientist and litterateur.

Mansfield, Katharine (1888–1923): English (actually New Zealander) writer, principally of short stories.

Marlowe, Christopher (1564–1593): Elizabethan poet, playwright, and possibly spy.

Marvell, Andrew (1621–1678): Known in his lifetime as a satirist and English patriot, his breathtaking lyric poems were all but ignored for more than two centuries after his death.

Marx, Groucho (1891–1977): A better comedian than gardener.

Marx, Leo (1919–   ): American social and cultural historian.

Mason, William (1725–1797): Eighteenth-century English literary man; among his on-the-whole-weak poems is a huge blank-verse epic on landscape gardening.

McGinley, Phyllis (1905–1977): Humorous poet, for many years a mainstay of *The New Yorker.*

Meynell, Alice (1847–1922): English poet and essayist.

Miller, Philip (1691–1771): For nearly half a century in charge of the Chelsea Physic Garden, Miller is remembered also for his magisterial *Dictionary of Gardening.* It remained a standard guide almost until modern times, going through many editions.

Milnes, Richard Monckton, Lord Houghton (1809–1885): Member of Parliament, biographer, literary editor, and collector of erotic books.

Milton, John (1608–1674): English epic poet.

Mitchell, Henry (1923–1993): Late gardening columnist in the *Washington Post* and author of three books, Mitchell is to my mind the most quotable of any writer included in this collection. I say this with a faint twinge of embarrassment; years ago, when I was an editor in New York and his first manuscript was going the rounds of publishers, *I turned it down!* Fortunately another publisher had more sense and foresight, and now Henry Mitchell's books are unlikely to go out of print for a long time. My only regret is that he's no longer around to write more of them.

Mitford, Mary Russell (1787–1855): Slightly saccharine novelist of English village life.

Mitford, Nancy (1904–1973): Novelist, best known of the four Mitford sisters.

Montagu, Lady Mary Wortley (1689–1762): Strong-minded, witty, and interesting woman, writer of brilliant letters and less brilliant poems. Introduced the practice of smallpox inoculation into England from Turkey.

Montaigne, Michel de (1533–1592): French essayist and man of reason.

Montesquieu, Charles-Louis de Secondat (1689–1755): French social and political philosopher, author of a famous study of constitutional law. His *Lettres Persanes* purport to be written by a Persian visitor to France.

Moore, Marianne (1887–1972): Distinctively quirky yet attractive poet, whose work is marked by precise and detailed observation. "I will admit," she once wrote to Ezra Pound, "that at times I am heady and irresponsible." This should not discourage anyone not familiar with her poems from becoming so.

Morris, James (1926–): British historian, journalist, and travel writer. Now known as Jan Morris since a sex-change operation.

Morris, William (1834–1896): Prolific English writer of verse and prose romances, political tracts, and other works, and— as a designer, architect, and theoretician—a key figure in the artistic life of the late nineteenth century.

Murasaki Shikibu (970?–1020?): Japanese court lady, author of the magnificent *Tale of Genji,* about whom very little is known. Even her real name is uncertain, although she was a member of the Fujiwara family, the most powerful in Japan at the time, and it is clear from her novel that she was intimately involved with the highest levels of the imperial court.

Nash, Ogden (1902–1971): American writer of sensationally unmetrical verse.

Nemerov, Howard (1920–): American poet.

Nichols, Beverley (1899–   ): English author of many mainly whimsical books, including several dealing with his gardening adventures. An acquired taste.

Osler, Mirabel: Writer of several elegant and amusing garden books; her best-known, *A Gentle Plea for Chaos*, deals mostly with a garden she and her husband built on a hillside in Shropshire.

Ou-yang Hsiu (1007–1072): The leading literary figure of his generation in China, known for the directness and simplicity of his verse.

Page, Russell (1906–1985): Prominent English garden designer and writer. He was responsible for a number of exceptional gardens in England and France, and his principal book, *The Education of a Gardener*, has been reprinted several times.

Parkinson, John (1567–1650): Royal botanist to Charles I, who suffered banishment and bemoaned the loss of his fine London garden during the Cromwellian interregnum. Parkinson's most famous book, the punningly titled *Paradisi in sole Paradisus terrestris* ("Park-in-sun's earthly paradise"), remains delightful reading.

Patmore, Coventry (1823–1896): English Catholic poet.

Peacock, Thomas Love (1785–1866): Brilliantly funny English satirical novelist, who made mock of—among many other things—the early nineteenth-century taste for picturesque landscape design.

Peele, George (1556–1596): Relatively unsuccessful Elizabethan playwright, who on occasion came up with passages of memorable beauty.

Perelman, S. J. (1904–1979): American humorist, the archetypical city dweller, who made the mistake of buying a farm. He then redeemed himself by writing about it.

Perényi, Eleanor (1918–   ): American writer and magazine editor, author of a biography of Liszt as well as a perfectly splendid collection of gardening essays, *Green Thoughts*, which I cannot recommend too highly.

Phillpotts, Eden (1862–1960): Long-lived English author of dozens of popular novels along with a gardening book or two.

Piozzi, Hester Lynch (1741–1821): Possibly better known as Mrs. Thrale, from her first marriage to the brewer Henry Thrale, she was a close friend of Samuel Johnson, and published a book of anecdotes about him.

Plath, Sylvia (1932–1963): Fine American poet, whose work has been overshadowed by the tragic story of her suicide; it should not be.

Po Chü-i (772–846): One of the most famous and loved of all Chinese poets.

Pollan, Michael: Of his lively and profound 1991 book *Second Nature,* which centers, with divagations, upon his garden in rural Connecticut, the *New York Times* reviewer was moved to say "I know no other book on gardening that is quite as illuminating and fascinating as this one." Strong words, but not far off the mark.

Pope, Alexander (1688–1774): Matchless English poet, satirist, and pace-setting gardener.

Pound, Ezra (1885–1972): Controversial American poet, whose work combines enormous beauty with the most vicious stupidity.

Proust, Marcel (1871–1922): French author of a huge—and hugely entertaining—novel, of which many readers know only the first volume or so. This is a pity.

Quarterly Review, The: One of the two most important literary and political journals of Victorian England (the other was *The Edinburgh Review*).

Raver, Anne (1949–   ): Gardening correspondent for *The New York Times* and author of a fetching 1995 book of essays on (mostly) gardening.

Reed, Christopher: American garden writer.

Repton, Humphry (1752–1818): Landscape designer responsible for restoring—albeit modestly—flowers to the English garden, after his predecessor "Capability" Brown had virtually banished them. Wrote rather dry books on design theory.

Rieu, E. V. (1887–1972): Longtime editor of the Penguin Classics series, several of which he translated himself. A writer of light verse by avocation.

Rilke, Rainer Maria (1875–1926): Greatest lyric poet in German of the twentieth century.

Robinson, William (1838–1935): Extremely influential English gardening journalist, responsible—with Gertrude Jekyll—for the modern informal style of garden design. In his books, in his magazine *The Garden,* and in the theories demonstrated in his own magnificent garden at Gravetye Manor in Sussex, Robinson spoke with vigor and success against Victorian carpet bedding and allied sins.

Rostand, Edmund (1868–1918): French playwright best known for his romantic recreation of the big-nosed seventeenth-century soldier-hero Cyrano de Bergerac.

Ruskin, John (1819–1900): Artist, art and social critic, tastemaker, prolific author.

Sackville-West, Victoria Mary (1892–1962): Poet and novelist who is probably best remembered, especially among gardeners, for creating (with her husband Harold Nicolson) Sissinghurst in Kent, arguably the finest garden in Great Britain today.

Saint-Simon, Duc de (1675–1755): French memoirist, notably of court life during the reign of Louis XIV. His account is lively and opinionated, a classic of the diarist's art.

Saltonstall, Wye: Minor seventeenth-century literary figure known mostly as a translator from Latin. There was a fashion for writing "characters" of stock types.

Sargent, Henry Winthrop (1810–1882): Wealthy Hudson River estate owner, neighbor and friend of Andrew Jackson Downing, with an interest in arboriculture. He updated and expanded Downing's treatise on landscape gardening after the latter's death.

Sarton, May (1912–1996): American poet and novelist, a feminist icon.

Scott, Frank J. (1828–1919): American writer on gardens and architecture.

Scott, Sir Walter (1771–1832): Novelist, poet, and devoted planter of trees.

Sei Shōnagon: Tenth-century Japanese court lady, a near contemporary of Murasaki Shikibu (*The Tale of Genji*) and author of one of the most delightful books in any language. Both funny and thoughtful, and filled with often startling perceptions, *The Pillow Book* was written about the year 1002 but could scarcely seem fresher had it been written a thousand years later.

Shakespeare, William (1564–1616): The English poet and dramatist.

Shaw, George Bernard (1856–1950): Profoundly argumentative English playwright, author of more than fifty plays, nearly all successful.

Shelley, Percy Bysshe (1792–1822): English poet, author of brilliant lyric verse as well as works of powerful intellectual originality. Died tragically young.

Shenstone, William (1714–1763): English poet and essayist, creator of a rural landscape garden called the Leasowes, near what is now Birmingham. He wrote garden poetry, and slightly pointless notes on the theory of garden design.

Sitwell, Sir George (1860–1943): Wealthy and eccentric English gentleman who built gardens on his estates in Derbyshire and Italy. His book on garden-making retains a faded charm.

Smart, Christopher (1722–1771): Fairly prolific but undistinguished poet during much of his lifetime, although during his confinement in an insane asylum he composed an extraordinary long unfinished poem, filled with brilliant lines and phrases drawn from a wide range of scientific, botanical, and religious sources, called *Jubilate Agno*. It was not published until nearly two hundred years after his death.

Smith, Adam (1723–1790): The father of economics.

Smollett, Tobias (1721–1771): English traveler, novelist, and controversialist.

Snyder, Gary (1930–   ): Beat Generation American poet much influenced by Japanese and Chinese models.

St. John, Henry, Lord Bolingbroke (1678–1751): English politician and historian.

Stein, Gertrude (1874–1946): American writer, settled in France, whose output of idiosyncratic poetry, fiction, and essays is never less than interesting, and sometimes dazzling.

Stein, Sara: American author of books for children as well as several fascinating works on natural history, especially weeds. Her writings, through their clarity and originality, have played a part in the modern movement toward natural gardening.

Sterne, Laurence (1713–1768): English novelist, primordial inventor of the "stream-of-consciousness" technique in his engaging masterwork *Tristram Shandy*, which has been called the world's longest shaggy-dog story.

Stevens, Wallace (1879–1955): American insurance executive, better known as a quirky, often enigmatic, intellectually challenging poet. A number of his poems deal with plants and gardens; they are among his best.

Stevenson, Robert Louis (1850–1894): Scottish writer, beset by ill health most of his life, who eventually died in Samoa, where he had gone in search of a more salubrious climate.

Stout, Ruth (1884–1980): Inventor of the Stout method of no-work gardening, which she practiced in her Connecticut garden. It involved spreading a permanent thick layer of hay mulch over the bed and planting through it, without digging. It works, for some people.

Strong, Roy: English art and cultural historian, former head of the National Portrait Gallery, who writes widely on garden history and design. He has created a sizable garden in Herefordshire, on the principle of making a series of separate garden "rooms."

Surtees, R. S. (1805–1864): Before inheriting an estate at the age of thirty-three and becoming a full-time English country squire, Surtees wrote eight highly successful novels revolving around his favorite pastime, fox-hunting.

Swinnerton, Frank (1884–1982): English critic and novelist. His output was huge; he published his last book at the age of ninety-four.

Tanizaki Junichiro (1886–1965): Japan's greatest modern novelist, author of dozens of varied works, possibly the most important— and engrossing—of which is *The Makioka Sisters.*

Temple, Sir William (1628–1699): Skilled English diplomat and gardener, author of essays, letters, and memoirs.

Thomas, Dylan (1914–1953): Welsh tippler and poet.

Thomas, Edward (1878–1917): Accurate and profound poet of the English natural scene. He began by writing biographies and topographical works to earn a living, until Robert Frost encouraged him to try poetry. Thomas was killed in France during the First World War.

Thoreau, Henry David (1817–1862): More a philosopher than a gardener, Thoreau knew enough, and saw keenly enough, to write some of the finest descriptions of plants and nature that we have. The detail and tangibility of his prose is uncanny.

Thurber, James (1894–1961): American humorist.

Trollope, Frances (1780–1863): Mother of the novelist William, and a writer herself, who traveled to America and wrote an acerb book called *Domestic Manners of Americans* (of which she most markedly disapproved).

Tusser, Thomas (1524–1580): Author of a collection of doggerel quatrains on farming, gardening, and housekeeping.

Twain, Mark (1835–1910): American humorist.

Virgil (70–19 B.C.): The greatest Roman poet, author—in addition to epics—of a celebration of Italian rural life, the *Georgics*.

Voltaire (1694–1778): French satirist, critic, novelist, playwright, etc. Author of *Candide*.

von Arnim, Countess Elizabeth (1866–1941): English novelist who married a German count. Her intermittently bad-tempered account of life on the family estate in Pomerania, *Elizabeth and Her German Garden*, is her best-known work.

Waller, Edmund (1606–1687): English courtier and poet, responsible for some exquisite lyrics.

Walpole, Horace (1717–1797): Rich, highly intelligent, and witty dilettante, author of reams of wonderful letters, and a highly influential essay *On Modern Gardening*, among other works. He built a famous house and garden at Strawberry Hill on the edge of London.

Warner, Charles Dudley (1829–1900): American journalist who would probably be wholly unknown today except for one extremely clever and funny little book called *My Summer in a Garden*.

Wells, H. G. (1866–1946): English novelist, virtual inventor of science fiction.

Wen Zhenheng (1585–1645): Chinese essayist and arbiter of taste in the late Ming Dynasty, author of *Treatise on Superfluous Things*, a guide intended to help rich people spend their money appropriately (including on gardens).

Wharton, Edith (1862–1937): American novelist and writer on gardens; she created a fine garden on the grounds of her mansion in Lenox, Massachusetts.

White, Gilbert (1720–1793): Curate of Selborne in Hampshire, where he was born and spent his life, and an amateur naturalist with brilliant powers of observation. His *Natural History of Selborne* is a classic, and a delight.

White, Katharine S.: American author of a single, wonderful book, *Onward and Upward in the Garden*, edited after her death by her husband E. B. White from articles first published in *The New Yorker*, where they both worked for many years.

White, Patrick (1912–1990): Novelist and savage critic of his native Australia, where in spite of everything he finally settled, bred dogs, and raised a garden.

Whitman, Walt (1819–1892): American poet.

Whittle, Tyler (1927–1994): Anglican clergyman (under his real name, Michael Sidney Tyler-Whittle) with parishes in Staffordshire and Kent, and author of many books, including a lively history of plant hunters and two books of essays on gardening.

Wilde, Oscar (1854–1900): Irish playwright and all-around wit.

Wilson, Colin (1931–   ): English writer, author of *The Outsider*, and many less successful books.

Wodehouse, P. G. (1881–1975): Possibly England's most widely read humorist, author of more than 120 books.

Wordsworth, William (1770–1850): English poet, whose work was both loved and admired, and bitterly attacked.

Wright, Frank Lloyd (1867–1959): American architect, centrally important figure with an ego to match.

Yeh Shao-weng: Late twelfth– early thirteenth–century Chinese poet and historian.

Young, Arthur (1741–1820): English agricultural writer and editor who also published descriptive books on Ireland and France.

Zola, Emile (1840–1902): Grimly downbeat French novelist whose works could unexpectedly contain passages of lyrical beauty.

Index of Those Quoted

ACKNOWLEDGMENTS

From *The Land*. Copyright Vita Sackville-West 1926, reproduced by permission of Curtis Brown Limited, London. "Roses Only": Reprinted with the permission of Simon & Schuster, from *Selected Poems Of Marianne Moore*. Copyright 1935 by Marianne Moore; copyright renewed © 1963 by Marianne Moore and T. S. Eliot. From *Patrick White Letters*, edited by David Marr, published by University of Chicago Press 1994. From *Blandings Castle*: Permission granted by A. P. Watt Ltd., on behalf of The Trustees of the P. G. Wodehouse Estate. Extract taken from a longer work. Excerpt from *Revenge of the Lawn*. Copyright © 1963, 1964, 1965, 1966, 1967, 1969, 1970, 1971 by Richard Brautigan. Reprinted by permission of Houghton Mifflin Co. All rights reserved. From "The Rose Family" from *The Poetry of Robert Frost*, edited by Edward Connery Lathem, © 1956 by Robert Frost. Copyright 1928, © 1969 by Henry Holt and Company, Inc. Reprinted by permission of Henry Holt and Company, Inc. From *The Pillow Book of Sei Shōnagon*, translated by Ivan Morris. Copyright © 1967 Columbia University Press. Reprinted with permission of the publisher. From *The Education of a Gardener* by Russell Page. Copyright © 1962 by Russell Page. Reprinted by permission of Random House, Inc. "Man with Pruning Shears," from *The Love Letters of Phyllis McGinley* by Phyllis McGinley. Copyright 1951, 1952, 1953, 1954 by Phyllis McGinley. Copyright renewed © 1979, 1980, 1981, 1982 by Phyllis Hayden Blake. 1982 by Phyllis Hayden Blake. Used by permission of Viking Penguin, a division of Penguin Putnam, Inc. "Bavarian Gardens" by D. H. Lawrence, from *The Complete Poems of D. H. Lawrence*, edited by V. de Sola Pinto & F. W. Roberts. Copyright © 1964, 1971 by Angelo Ravagli and C. M. Weekley, Executors of the Estate of Frieda Lawrence Ravagli. Used by permission of Viking Penguin, a division of Penguin Putnam, Inc. From *Province of the Heart* by Phyllis McGinley. Copyright © 1959 by Phyllis McGinley, renewed 1987 by Patricia Hayden Blake. Used by permission of Viking Penguin, a division of Penguin Putnam, Inc. "A Room on a Garden": From *Opus Posthumous* by Wallace Stevens, ed., Samuel French Morse. Copyright © 1957 by Elsie Stevens and Holly Stevens. Reprinted by permission of Alfred A. Knopf, Inc. "A Room on a Garden": From *Opus Posthumous* by Wallace Stevens, ed., Samuel French Morse. Copyright © 1957 by Elsie Stevens and Holly Stevens. Reprinted by permission of Faber & Faber. From "Credences of Summer": From *Collected Poems by Wallace Stevens*. Copyright © 1947 by Wallace Stevens. Reprinted by permission of Alfred A. Knopf, Inc. Excerpt from "Credences of Summer": From *Collected Poems by Wallace Stevens*. Copyright © 1947 by Wallace Stevens. Reprinted by permission of Faber & Faber. "Rhododendrons" by Ted Hughes: From *New Selected Poems 1957–1994 by Ted Hughes*, published in 1995. Copyright © 1995 by Ted Hughes. Reprinted by permission of Faber & Faber. From *Plant Dreaming Sleep* by May Sarton. Copyright © 1968 by May Sarton. Reprinted by permission of W. W. Norton & Company, Inc. From *My Weeds* by Sara Stein.